The Masters of the S
Selections from their blo

Spirit World Wisdom

Channeled by
Toni Ann Winninger

Selected and edited by
Peter Watson Jenkins

~ *Celestial Voices* ~

Spirit World Wisdom

Note about this collection of essays
All the messages in this book were first published on behalf of the Masters by Celestial Voices, Inc. from 1 August 2007 to 31 December 2010 on the blog:

www. mastersofthespiritworld.com.

Contents

Most of the Spirit Masters' messages were originally framed in answer to questions posed by readers. Arrangement of these messages into chapters and sections gives readers a general guide to the content. In this book, the Masters' words are printed in roman type. *Editorial comment and notes are printed in italic type.*

Acknowledgment

Sonia Ness our copy editor
for her good work

The Spirit Masters'
Introduction

Introduction

Welcome! We are glad that you are reading our book. Let us start by telling you about ourselves. None of us in our ever-changing group of enlightened, ascended masters is currently engaged in physical experience on planet Earth. Some of us have ascended from physical form, having learned from all the experiences we chose to have as human beings. While we are deciding whether to return for further lessons, we offer assistance to you who are immersed in your own third-dimensional Earth lessons. Some of us are celestial beings who have never incarnated on the Earth plane—whom you have historically referred to as angels and archangels.

We have acted for years as the personal guides of our channel, Toni Ann Winninger, though other guides come to assist her when a matter needing their expertise is being discussed. We recruited this physical channel because of her ease in translating vibrational energy language. We sought a human voice that contained a broad base of experience and information so we could use complicated concepts to provide a depth and fluidity to our communications.

We arranged to have a website in order to assist you who are contained in a physical form to accomplish your various Earth lessons and life missions. We do this as an expression of the unconditional love in which we exist. This book contains some of the messages that have been posted on our website during the first three-and-a-half years of its existence. We asked Toni and her colleagues Peter Watson Jenkins and Sonia Ann Ness to assist us with this publication.

Our weblog "mastersofthespiritworld.com" allows you to post your own questions. We encourage you to become personally involved. Please pass on this information to your family and friends so that they may read our messages. We hope you will enjoy this book and the various electronic means we are using to communicate with you, including our Facebook site, "Reincarnation Guide."

Awareness

More and more of you are starting to *feel* where you are and to know the intended contracts and pathways you had envisioned for this incarnation. It is enjoyable for us to witness this transformation within a human being: first being totally controlled by the conscious mind/ego on the Earth plane, determining everything by judgment; then converting this experience into a life of feeling from the heart and soul, which educates your soul for all eternity. We urge you to be steadfast in your progress. Be open to whatever you are bringing to yourself for experience. Live in the present without spending much valuable time on the past or the future. Relish each experience and learn everything that is possible from each situation.

We are always here to help when needed. But lest you forget, we cannot make decisions for you. You have total freedom of choice to determine the way you learn each lesson. Evaluate each experience to see if you want to take the learning further in that area, or if you have had quite enough just as it is. The choice is yours!

The Masters' language

We want now to define what we mean by some of the terms that we use in this book. We are aware that your language is imprecise in the understanding of some similar words. We also know that some human teachers have adopted and adapted words and phrases which for us have commonly understood concepts, and these teachers have assigned meanings to them that differ from ours. So, because we do not wish our explanations to be misunderstood by you, we have chosen to begin with a few definitions.

We do not speak in the vocabulary of organized religion because religions are constructs in your world to provide guidelines on how to conduct your lives. We know that all souls have freedom of choice to experience whatever they feel can best teach them what they need to learn. We begin with just a few words that are the essence of our message and our existence.

Creator, God, God-Force, Holy Spirit, Source: These terms, and many more, all refer to the point of origin of all that is known by you, and all that exists.

Source (or any of the above regularly used terms in this genre—feel free to use them interchangeably): This is the energy of unconditional love and, when viewed in your judgmental way, of perfection. Source itself makes no judgments; therefore, nothing is right or wrong but is simply whatever experience the soul seeks to undertake.

Everything within that which you call the universe, and within the entirety of your human understanding, is energy, and energy is everything. Source is the highest vibrational energy anywhere and is found in everything. It permeates all that exists but does not interfere with or prevent the soul from having physical experiences.

Source created souls so it could learn all about itself through understanding what it was not. Source is unconditional love. Everything that is not uncompromising, unconditional love adds information and eventually wisdom to the experience of existence. In order to learn, it is necessary to start from a place of having no information. This is accomplished by the incarnate soul's starting with amnesia as to its true identity.

Souls: When Source wanted to experience other aspects of existence that were not perfect or not unconditional love, the only way to do so was to split off parts of itself into individualized pieces of energy that could have distinctive experiences outside the perfect. We refer to these separate pieces as souls, but remember they are all pieces of Source, so each and every soul is also Source. We address you as "fellow souls" because we originated from Source in the same fashion as you did and share the distinction of being divisions of Source.

All parts of Source are the same, even though some have chosen to have varying types of human experiences. All souls are equal regardless of the human "shell" they have chosen to inhabit. No one soul is any better than any other because no one piece of Source is any better than any other. Is a finger or toe of your body any more important or better than any other?

Home: Within modern religious understanding this may be equated with Heaven, Nirvana, Sheol, Tian, Swarga Loka, The Garden of Eden, or Paradise. When a soul finishes each lifetime of lessons it returns Home. Initially this feels to the soul like the womb of its remembered physical sensitivities. But Home is not a physical place; it is an energetic dimension of unconditional love and of conscious connection with Source.

Returning Home involves reintegration into the matrix of all energy, where the lessons recently experienced can be examined and shared with all, in order to incorporate the wisdom of each distinct part into the whole. It is a place where each soul works with its guides, and frequently with its council, to see if it has truly learned the lessons it chose or if it will have to reincarnate in order to fully understand the lesson. Every soul who is not incarnated in a physical form is consciously within the dimension of Home.

The Spirit Masters

If you are unfamiliar with the Spirit Masters' language, you may find it useful to review the Glossary at the end of the book.

Spirit World Wisdom

Chapter One
Masters & Guides

In this chapter the Spirit Masters discuss the contact human beings may have with personal guides; a variety of other guides, including the Masters themselves; currently incarnate souls; and discarnate souls.

Contact with the Masters
Contacting spirit guides
Masters on Earth
Able to believe
When angels incarnate
Channeling explained
Communicating with spirits
Abraham and the Spirit Masters
Other channeled spirits
Language barriers
Automatic writing
Psychic practices
Channeling a living person
Psychic accuracy
Universal energy
Where do the Masters live?
Life as a spirit

Contact with the Masters

All souls—the fundamental energy contained within each and every being—originated and broke off from a single Source. For this reason, no being is any more important than, better than, or less than, any other.

Titles are very important on your planet to give you direction. You label everything to save time. You have doctors, dentists, lawyers, teachers, and government officials. If you did not have labels you would spend precious time, say, talking to a teacher before you learned she was not the dentist that you needed for your abscessed tooth. We choose to be referred to as Masters of the Spirit World—we are non-physical, enlightened beings [spirits] who wish to offer our services to your society in any way that is meaningful to you.

We are everywhere, in everything. It is as easy for a miner working deep in the bowels of the Earth to talk with us as it is for an astronaut in space. It is only necessary to rid oneself of distractions and go into the quiet of one's soul or inner self to be in conversation with any of us. We have small, silent voices compared to the blaring television set or mp3 player, or the cacophony of traffic and industrial noises.

To hear us you must first be able to listen to your own thoughts, to go into the silence within, as the monks say. So wherever you can bring yourself into that quiet, you can be with us; time and space will not aid your quest. Please come and visit us often.

When we talk about the universe in its broadest terms, we are referring to everything that exists in all dimensions, times, and energies, such as thoughts, vibrations, and sounds. When we speak of the universe as distinguished from one specific person, we refer to everything that is not that individual energy. This is frequently accepted to be the totality of all other energy outside that one soul. Many call this the Source, or the God-Force, which is part and parcel of all souls and all existence.

Contacting spirit guides

Contacting your spirit guides is easier than you think. The crucial issue in understanding the way guides may assist you is to be aware of the way *you* choose to interact with them. Back Home, before you entered your current body, your council, a group of twelve advisors, helped you to decide exactly what you wanted to experience in this particular life. Together you reviewed those lessons you had not yet learned or completed, but which you wished to incorporate into your wisdom. You visualized how it would best serve you to undertake these lessons, and you decided with whom you needed to have contracts to ensure that you would be confronted with situations needed for each lesson.

Once you had finalized your plan, having personally chosen the type of environment you needed—including the time of your birth, your parents, siblings, health status, and so on—you entered into your chosen body and began your learning process. With all these well-laid plans, the only problem for you was that you came down to Earth with amnesia and now have no idea why you are here!

Before embarking upon your journey, you chose and agreed with other souls to have them available to assist you. Your choice of guides may be constant throughout your lifetime, but it's more likely that you selected various experts to accompany you into new areas of learning.

Even with all these arrangements in place, the fact is that you are now physical while the guides remain energetic, so they cannot assist you as planned unless you actually *request* their help while in physical form. For them to intervene in your life, just because you had arranged for their assistance before you came into a body, is insufficient. As at all times, when in physical form we all have freedom to change our mind.

So now you find yourself in a pickle and can't decide what to do about some troublesome lesson that's facing you.

You've consulted all your friends, prayed for outside intervention (so you don't have to take responsibility for your actions), and now you think of *them.* Those, possibly mythical, guides and guardian angels are *supposed* to help you out—but you don't know how to contact them. What can you do?

The answer is to ask for our assistance with the clear understanding that, because we cannot interfere with your freedom of choice, we cannot tell you exactly what you should do. We can support you, and we can let you see both the benefits of the pathway you are currently traveling and alternatives that are open to you.

How are you to "hear" us? We place the word "hear" in quotation marks because we do not have vocal cords, so you cannot actually hear us speak with a distinctive voice. We communicate in vibrations that are somewhat like your unseen radio waves. These are then translated into thoughts or actions that are understandable to you.

You must be fully aware and observant of the things around you in order to receive our messages. We use many things that can be perceived by your senses as signs for you to affirm your decisions. A very popular way for us to help you is giving you dreams that show you pathways. We also use things in nature—animals, birds, weather, lightning— and even objects such as billboards, bells, writing on trucks, familiar scents, and numbers.

Say you are asking us for assistance to decide if it will be right for you to change your employment. Then you see that the clock reads 11:11, a symbol for the beginning of a venture. You are wondering if you really have the necessary background to take a new educational course, and you *hear* an unequivocal *voice* in your head saying "Go for it!" You will question this voice because it sounds like your own thinking—but then why wouldn't it? We don't have voices to speak to you, so our energetic vibrations, when converted by you to be understood, will sound exactly like your own voice. The best way to test this is to get out of your head and go into your heart and ask yourself, "Does it feel truthful to me?"

Everything that is stored in your head has been put there by others outside of you. These are all things that people told you, or which you read. They are other people's opinions. But when you go inside, and ask your heart and soul, you are tapping into your essence. It comes from the wisdom you have gathered in this life, and in your previous lives, and is your personal truth. Feel the rightness of these contacts; then you will be certain that you are being assisted by your guides. We encourage you to consult us frequently. We love to interact with you during your quiet periods, such as in meditation. We are always here.

Masters on Earth

A master is a soul who has learned everything there is to know about a particular life lesson. This generally comes after a number of different physical lives during which the soul has explored the lesson from all its various angles and possible manifestations. Most masters do not stop with just learning about a single life lesson. They will spend many lives, several of your centuries, gleaning knowledge about their Earth-based experiences which they can turn into wisdom.

Having spent multiple lives gaining wisdom, a master then enters into service helping other souls to understand the nature of the human experience as a tool for truly appreciating their magnificence as part of Source. Most masters perform this guidance from the confines of Home— as a personal guide to an incarnate soul, as a member of an individual soul's council, or as part of a debriefing team when a soul is newly returned.

11

During the developmental phase of the human experiment, masters frequently walked the Earth because personal contact was the only way to interact with other souls. No media of any kind existed. History was oral and at the whim of the teller. Patterns for humanity had to be established. The Buddha, Mohammad, and Jesus were some of the masters who came to your Earth to teach about truth, discipline, and compassion, and to set standards of behavior. They are those who show the way.

In your time, the work of the masters is well documented. Their examples and teachings may be found everywhere, if you look. There is no need for a new master to appear to show the way. The directions and pathways are there for all to see.

This is a time for action, not a time to sit and study at the feet of a master. With the instructions they have left you it is possible to go inside and reconnect with your true essence, which is the purpose of your life on Earth.

There are many masters walking the face of the planet, but they are not there to emulate the practices of old. They are simply with you to help you feel the energy of the Source more easily so that you may find the mastery within yourself. They choose not to reveal themselves because they do not want students who blindly follow. It is a time for each soul to find its own strength, power, and majesty.

Able to believe

We are constantly hearing requests from humans that they need to see us so that they can know themselves and what they need to do. They want to physically hear us so they can be told if they are doing what they should.

First, we will not show ourselves just so you can believe we are real, and we will never tell you what to do because that would interfere with your freedom of choice and we may not do that. Second, we ask why you need to see us. Is it that you do not believe we exist? Or despite feeling that we do exist, do you still require physical validation?

We are energy and do not appear to people unless there is a very good reason. We do not communicate in your vocal language unless you are so disbelieving as to need to hear from outside yourself. But normally we do not bother because you would simply find some physical explanation for the phenomenon you observe.

Our usual means of communication uses vibrations— whereby we stimulate the centers of your brain that translate and record messages from outside you. What you perceive is the sound of your own voice telling you the advice you seek, or the innate knowing that a particular fact is true.

You need to have faith in yourself and the feelings that you detect from within. We are always helping you; we will not make your decisions for you, but we give you facts that will allow you to make an informed decision for yourself.

When angels incarnate

Not all souls who start out their existence as angels—those who choose to act from Home as guides for souls having a human experience—remain at Home. Once guides have watched and helped other souls to learn lessons, and to experience emotions and physical experiences that can only be had in the duality of Earth, most of them want to have experiences of their own.

When a soul who has spent time as an angel decides to have a physical experience, it comes into its body with the same degree of amnesia shared by all other souls. In order to learn from a lesson it has the same pattern of being confronted by a test, using its freedom of choice to work through the test, and gathering the knowledge the experience allows it. It is working through the same types of lessons as all other souls, so even an angel can be a nasty, deceitful, hateful individual. That does not remove the energy signature at a deeper level of what it has done in the past. Psychics may be able to pick up the residue of its angelic work.

Channeling explained

Let us tell you a little about channeling. There are several different physical techniques channelers or mediums may use when delivering our messages.

Trance channelers, who are completely unconscious during the event, give their body and vocal cords over to our spiritual energy, have no input of their own at all in the process, and have no memory whatsoever of what has transpired.

Psychic channelers get information placed into their conscious or subconscious mind by the energies on the Other Side. As they do not have direct contact with us, they repeat the information as they interpret it.

Finally, pure or clear channels consciously step out of the way as our vibrational energy is coming through, and are merely receivers who translate our information into human-speak. The accuracy of this translation depends on the channel's own expertise in our vibrational language, partially based on information in their encyclopedia of knowledge from their experiences in this life and past lives.

A channel is just that—a conduit through which information flows without interference. Realize that some tubes are solid like PVC piping, while others have holes, and some are even made out of mesh or webbing.

The point of origin is an additional factor. Within the spirit world this involves the levels of the vibrational energy of the parties involved. In order to get a clear reception of an energy with vibrations as high as those of the Archangel

Michael, a channel must also vibrate at a very high level, without being held down by Earth-baggage.

Think of a radio. If your radio tuner is slightly off the right frequency, you may still be able to hear a program, but it is not clear and it fades in and out. Spiritual energies are the same. Conversing with a recently deceased soul, who has not totally severed its most recent bond with Earth, does not require the channel's energy level to be as high as that needed for interacting with an archangel.

Almost all of those who state they have obtained messages from Archangel Michael did in fact have them originate with him. A few psychics desperately want to hear from Michael but cannot step out of their own way to allow it. They may make something up, envisioning what they think he might want to say to you.

Conflicting information issues arise from variations in the purity of the flow of energy. If there is no interference from the human psyche or conscious mind, if channelers are in tune with the vibrations, and if they have a facility for translating the language of spiritual energy adequately, then all their messages will be identical. However, if anything fuzzes up the stream of energy, the messages become garbled or inconsistent. As with all things spiritual, we encourage you to see how a message *feels* to you before you accept it into your being. Channeling is a wonderful way to exchange information and teaching between the dimensions—but we are a bit prejudiced in that regard!

Archangel Michael wants everyone to know that he communicates with tens of thousands of people on a regular basis and helps millions throughout each of your calendar years. How is this possible, you ask? Michael, like all souls, being completely energetic, connects with the matrix that encompasses all energy and so can be everywhere all at once. This is not unusual but Michael has it down to a science and spends all his time putting out fires for people all over the planet. Don't hesitate to ask for his assistance when you need it—he promises he will be there for you.

Communicating with spirits

Inter-dimensional communication with spirit guides and with deceased relatives and friends is becoming accepted and honored in print and on television. Haven't you become aware of catching sight of movement out of the corner of your eyes? Did you speculate on that movement you saw the other night in the evening sky? Plain and simple—you are not alone in the universe.

Next question: who can and who cannot see? To be able to see and recognize anything, first you must accept that it can or does exist. You drive down the same streets every day and think you see what you have always seen. Then a friend calls your attention to a new structure, and you are flabbergasted that someone has been able to sneak in and erect a whole building overnight!

You did not "see" it while it was being erected because, to you, the space was an abandoned warehouse and nothing more. If you are always used to seeing emptiness, all you will see is emptiness. But if you believe something else might be there, you open yourself to seeing what else is there. You saw nothing new until your friend awakened in you the realization that the warehouse had been replaced. Then you saw it as it is now, not how it used to be.

To join the group of "seers," you need to believe that within the vastness of your physical universe there are any number of planets that have inhabitants. Accept that, just as people from different parts of the Earth have differing appearances, beings from a different planet will look different. The vehicles that are used for transport on different continents of planet Earth vary, and so will vehicles that are used to travel through space.

16

Abraham and the Spirit Masters

Abraham, channeled by Esther Hicks, is a group of souls just as we are. Some members of Abraham are also members of Masters of the Spirit World. If you take all of the messages from both groups as a whole, you will see they are not different but approach life lessons from different perspectives.

Abraham deals with day-to-day activities. The group emphasizes that all souls can create their own reality and that your essence, which is unconditional love, allows you to choose joy, freedom, and growth—if you make those the beliefs by which you live your life. This message is about positive reinforcement (such as affirmations) to rid your self of negativity and to allow the possibility for a happy life. In the same way that you need junior and high school to prepare yourself for entering the working world, you need to do this first before you can move on with life.

We specialize in going deeper into the behind-the-scenes spiritual growth program each soul comes to Earth to complete. This would be college or post-graduate information and theory that only those spending time on enlightenment need understand. We inform our readers of the Journey of the Soul and the steps each soul goes through before incarnating, and on Earth as a human being. Our biggest message is that, regardless of what souls planned to experience in this lifetime, they have complete freedom of choice what to do and how to complete their tasks.

If you want to be wealthy in a lifetime during which you wished to learn about poverty, you must first understand what the lack of money means to you (your life lesson) before you can move on to handling money as wealth. In this case, the search for abundance *is* the lesson you are studying. It is only when you believe you should do without money, and forget Abraham's teaching about manifestation, that you cannot shed the mantle of poverty.

Other channeled spirits

Elias, Seth, Abraham, Kryon, White Eagle, and many more entities have assumed a direct role in guiding humanity. The role of each is to provide information that will stimulate the group that they are impacting at a level that enables the recipients' growth, and their understanding of themselves as souls and of their place in the universe.

These entities each work in a unique manner. Some insert themselves into the situation by entering the channel in a trance state; others come through directly with the full awareness of the channel. Some work individually, and some come in groups. Whatever the manner of their presence, their message is what will be best received by the audience involved. The older the material, the more rigid it is, conforming to the structure expected in former days of information based on higher belief. It has the feel of a learned professor lecturing from a rostrum, using endearing words, sometimes even showing understanding of listeners' childish inexperience and lack of knowledge.

Modern messages are lighter, taking into consideration that the pre-eminent mission of the soul is to realize that all learning is effected through its exercise of free choice. For this reason, our messages, and those of some contemporaries, are not demanding, demeaning, or unequivocal; rather, they point out the options available for choices to be made. All these messages acknowledge the soul's powers, which are the first step to its awareness of self.

The mission we as a group have undertaken is to illuminate and inform, not to control nor to direct action. We will never tell people they must do something, because that takes away their freedom of choice. And now that the awareness of our divine non-physical guidance is being accepted, we are also bringing the message of enjoying this process you are going through with love, light, and laughter.

We come with total openness and the advice that our message may not be right for all people at this time. See how the information in this book resonates with you; if you are not ready today, put it on the shelf for tomorrow.

Language barriers

We are pleased that our books are creating spiritual questions as we had intended. You must look at the whole situation of communication from the perspective of a soul and not from the limitations of a human. Souls, in their purest form, are nothing but energy—an amorphous, cloud-like mass. They do not have languages, speech capabilities, or even a means to create sound. They communicate with vibrational energy sent from themselves to a receiver.

If the receiver is a human body, it may only translate the vibrations with capabilities within its own storehouse. In the first book in which we assisted, which contained questions to be asked of souls at Home, the soul of Adolf Hitler did not use any particular language, as you understand them, to send the vibrational thoughts to our channel Toni. The vibrations could be interpreted by Toni only within her range of knowledge. She is not fluent in German so the vibrations translated into English, which is her native tongue.

It is possible on some occasions for a non-physical to speak to a physical medium in a language with which the medium is not familiar. This can occur only if the non-physical energy comes down into the density of the Earth so that it is putting its human language into the mind or ears of the medium. Toni does not choose to use those means of contacting souls, but rather works almost exclusively with vibrational communications.

Automatic writing

What have you been thinking auto-writing is? That some being comes in and takes over your hand and scribbles its gibberish onto a piece of paper? Well, that *could* happen if you actually allowed it. Most auto-writing will start gently with basic messages. To allay your fears, before beginning any session, proclaim to the universe that you wish to communicate only with beings of the light and only for the highest and greatest good of the recipients of the messages received.

Your sessions can be as easy as a talk with your guides—but in written rather than oral form. Have a piece of paper and a pen or pencil (or sit in front of a computer if that feels better), clear your mind, and ask a question. Wait until your hand or fingers start formulating a response. It is very important that you get your thinking mind out of the way so it does not interfere. This may not work in the beginning. You must have patience. All of human life is regulated by the soul's freedom of choice. For that reason you are always at the position along your life's mission that you need to be when you are there.

Psychic practices

In the hands of an experienced practitioner, the various practices that questioners have mentioned to us—fortune telling, such as i-ching; face-features analysis; palm analysis; bazi analysis; and poker-card reading—can give an insight into the way that energy is flowing around a particular person or event. They can give you an historical perspective of how, in that specific setting, and with your particular background, you have had your life play out. That is true *for the moment of the reading*, until you or other people involved in your life exercise freedom of choice to change the way you or they had planned to act.

Since each person is unique, and experiences life with a different set of souls from those portrayed in history, the actual events can only give you a propensity for something to occur, but not a certainty. What you are obtaining is an indication of the direction of the energy flow around you. Does it not always help to be able to see which way the current is flowing so that you may take advantage of it and expend less energy to get somewhere?

Practitioners are as varied as the leaves on a tree—no two are the same. There is no way to say that the readers you have been exposed to are all open enough to sense and report the intricate energy streams they use within their crafts. It is for you to open yourself to their energy. See if they feel open to you; test to make sure they are not inputting their particular prejudices. How does what they are saying feel to you inside? If you resonate with the reading it is accurate for you, but don't let your desires for an outcome color the way you interpret the results.

Channeling a living person

Can a channeler talk to a facet of a soul while the focus of that soul is in a physical body? Yes, under some circumstances.

Is it also possible for a channeler to talk to the soul of a person in order for that person's conscious mind to learn about the soul's past and therefore understand what its current lessons are and why those particular lessons were chosen? No.

A channeler talking to an aspect of a soul currently involved in a physical life can only communicate with that person's higher self or unconscious memory. This can occur only with the permission of the soul because each soul has total freedom of choice concerning its essence.

The most common example of this kind of communication is a healer wishing to send healing to an incapacitated person from whom permission cannot be obtained directly. The channeler can then ask the patient's soul if it is all right for the healer to send energy to rebalance the body. If permission is not obtained, the healer is wasting time in sending energy because that energy cannot intervene without permission.

In the second scenario the soul came down to Earth with amnesia to learn lessons in the flesh. Had it wanted to have a memory of the why and wherefore of its lessons, it would have allowed itself to remember. This is a situation in which people may choose to engage in hypnotherapy to work through those lessons they have not completed or are having difficulty finishing.

Psychic accuracy

Messages that come through from the energetic plane are subject to interpretation by those who deliver them. We do not communicate in unequivocally understandable language; rather, we convey thoughts, pictures, and sensations that have to be translated into your language.

The degree to which the receiver can eliminate personal thoughts and just repeat ours indicates how accurate the reading will be. No person who is translating ideas from the Other Side is 100% accurate all the time.

There is another influence that affects the accuracy of readings. It has to do with the wisdom that readers have about spiritual matters so that they can interpret our sayings. When receivers color the information we provide with their own incorrect beliefs as to what life is like on the Other Side, the readings cannot then be accurate.

The last, but definitely not the least important, factor is whether the receivers are making sure that they are talking only to souls of the light and not to discarnate souls who have left their bodies but still inhabit the Earth plane. These beings generally love to make people miserable because they themselves have not returned to the unconditional love of Home and want others to feel lost as they are.

Universal energy

The majority of writings that speak about the Law of Attraction are trying to appeal to the mainstream, average citizens who need to have a belief in something because their world is not to their liking and they need to believe it can be changed.

A lot of the general public still take part in organized religion, or are those who believe in a god outside of themselves who is required to change things for them and to satisfy their needs and desires. These books and people are substituting the word "universe" to imply a god-source or divine presence outside of and different from the people themselves.

We say that the soul attracts to itself what it needs to experience for its growth and to understand its own nature. Everything that exists is energy. The conscious aspect of this energy is universal, all knowing, all seeing, always present, and magnificent in every facet since its point of origin is the initial spark of energy in the cosmos that religions call God and we refer to as Source energy.

Everything comes from this Source energy, which is, in totality, called "universal energy." All souls, and everything else that exists, are composed of this universal energy since they, at one time, were a part of that mass. When you intentionally call to yourself a needed experience, the circumstances to provide that event are brought to you by the energy around you—universal energy if you like—which includes your higher self and your guides, since all are a part of the everything.

Where do the Masters live?

The simple answer is anywhere and everywhere. The majority of us are exclusively in our soul form. Everyone's soul form is energetic and a part of the universal life force connective. Most of us do not choose to take a form similar to a human body so that we are free to be everywhere at once. When you take a body, you are stuck using a great deal of your energy to maintain that form so it is visible to others. Without such restriction we are free.

Certain of us Masters have a particular place on Earth— usually where we spent a lot of time while incarnate—which we frequent with our energy signature. This may be referred to as a "seat," or sometimes "retreat." Our energy is detectable at these locations to those humans who are sensitive, and our focus remains near so that we can immediately hear and respond to any request. This is really immaterial, though, because we can be felt at any place, by anyone, simply by being summoned to assist.

We are, first and foremost, guides to help you experience your life lessons while on Earth. Each of us has mastered some or all of the various categories of lessons (physical emotions) that are peculiar to Earth. We will not tell you what to do but will help you see your choices. We cannot, however, do this without being asked for assistance. Phrase your questions with care—we take them very literally!

Life as a spirit

Human bodies are very labor intensive. You have to feed, bathe, exercise, and love them—sounds almost like a pet, right? Our essence—container if you wish to compare it to a body—doesn't have a set form. It expands, contracts, divides, and morphs at will.

We can rejoin the Source from which we came, choose to be observant of multiple places at the very same moment, or reenter a human shell for yet another go at learning life lessons in the duality of planet Earth. We can also choose to enter into another life form and follow its requirements. The possibilities are limitless because we, the same as you, have total freedom of choice.

So, let's see, we were asked how we are sustained. We exist on a very simple substance, which inhabits the entirety of existence: unconditional love. Many also refer to it as universal energy, the same substance that healers use to heal, rebalance, and re-energize your human bodies. That is the substance we need, and the driving force is our sentience.

Chapter Two
Journey of the soul

The reason for our being on Earth is complex, but we feel an inner urge to know what it is. The Masters explore the answer to this question and consider variations in the life of the soul as it seeks to fulfill the quest of Source for a complete understanding of its nature. They also fill in some details of our soul journey that are of interest.

Purpose in life
The reason for reincarnation
The dualistic world
Understanding origin
The need for many lives
Life contracts
Karma
Spirit or soul?
Life after death
Responsibility
Souls and gender
Indigo and crystal children
Is romance necessary?

Purpose in life

We constantly get the question, "What is my purpose in life?" in some variation. Everyone feels that there must be one and only one purpose for their incarnating. When you were planning for a trip to Earth, however, you met with your council of advisors and discussed what lessons you wanted to learn. Your "purpose" is your reason for incarnating. This purpose is almost never a single thing you endeavor to experience but a series of things.

Once you enter into your human body you begin on your predetermined path, starting from the circumstances you had yourself born into, such as your birth family, whether the country was at peace or war, the family's monetary condition, your sex and race. You further had preplanned contracts that were made with other souls to allow you to see different sides of living, which would appear at an appropriate time in your life.

One thing is certain: the one purpose you *always* incarnate with is to find what it is that you wanted to accomplish. If we told you the specifics of each lesson you had decided to do, you would be missing half the process. When you were in school, if the teacher just told you the answers to the questions without asking the questions, you would learn nothing. For us to tell you what purpose you had in mind would be the same. In other words, discovering your purpose is always part of your purpose.

The reason for reincarnation

In the beginning was the magnificent, unconditionally loving, all-powerful, all-knowing Source. It was composed of all the energy that existed. In retrospect it has frequently been called "The One" or "Oneness." To be able to appreciate its magnitude, it had to understand and gain the wisdom of what it was *not*, what we call the negative aspect of each of its wonderful characteristics.

All Source knew was what it could experience in its own majesty: unconditional love. It wanted to learn more of how wonderful it was, and the only way to do that was to break off pieces of itself and let them experience what it was not, which would allow Source to experience their knowledge vicariously.

Source needed to create a place that had all the elements that were not unconditional love, so that it might feel and sense the differences. Earth was created for this purpose, so souls could take turns subjecting themselves to every possible condition that is not unconditional love.

In order to retain its extraordinary quality and still learn of negativity, it split minute pieces of itself into fact-finding bundles that are called "souls." All of these souls have their own memories and consciousness to provide the Oneness with the information they glean from their trips to Earth. They are continuously connected to Source but, when incarnate, do not have an awareness of that fact. Once an Earth mission is complete, they return to their energetic state and, once again, have total knowledge of the One, and enjoy the feeling of being the One—a journey of reunification.

The knowledge souls record from their experiences goes into a communal database shared by all. As souls tap into this data, it is like reading an historical text. They learn more about each experience and their sense of Source, and so their own essence evolves.

Gathering knowledge to learn the wisdom contained within an experience is the ultimate purpose of souls' coming to Earth. For each soul the path is different. One soul will undertake a seemingly simple lesson while another will engage in all the possible complexities of the same general lesson. It all has to do with the maturity of the soul and how many previous times it has incarnated.

Souls enter into a physical body in order to learn lessons and enrich their knowledge of life. This is easily accomplished by the ability to use any body form available to them. They generally do not like to repeat something they have already learned, so they will move into other environments to vary their knowledge base. Every soul who has chosen to come to Earth a number of times has been male and female, white, black, oriental, and indigenous native, choosing to live on a number of different continents experiencing myriad families and occupations.

The dualistic world

Earth was created to be different from every other physical location. Its appeal to the learning process of the soul is its polarity. The soul's choice to come to Earth is to experience life within polarity, or state of negativity, which cannot be found anywhere else.

Each soul does not choose to experience everything, all in one lifetime. Many things may be occurring on the planet when they are there, but they will not participate in any more than they are capable of learning from at that time.

Your soul may choose to go to other places than Earth to have a life. Even within this polarity you may have plenty of happiness upon Earth if you complete the lessons you came to learn and remember your true nature—which is unconditional love.

Understanding origin

The soul contained within each human body has its point of origin from the Source. Some souls seek to take a physical form when various planets are first populated. Others choose to wait until a community or society has evolved on a planet for the purpose of allowing souls to understand different types of existence. Some places were created to experience a different type of energy, where the soul takes a convenient body form to align with energies such as air, earth, water, or fire. Other places offer interactive social experiences that are non-judgmental and cover such tasks as advisor, manager, worker, intellectual, or peacemaker. Some souls may want to be warriors, athletes, physically or mentally challenged people, or simply observers.

The fact that a soul chose one particular characteristic as its initial life form did not prohibit it from then going into something totally different at the completion of the first lifetime. Whatever part your soul chose at that specific period in time did not restrict you to one definition for your other trips to Earth. Remember that each incarnation is merely a role that you have chosen to portray for a little part of your existence. You are eternal, beginning with your soul's division from Source. Knowing a particular role you took [e.g., through hypnosis] only tells you what particular skills you may have mastered.

It is best to go inside and ask yourself, "What skills do I know I have brought into this life to use for myself and others?" Knowing that you have visited a country does not make you an expert in that country's customs unless you engaged in every possible combination available. Rarely does a soul take the time to learn other than that which it has chosen to come and learn. If you are of early Roman lineage in one of your lives, it does not mean you can now speak Italian.

The need for many lives

The consciousness of the soul is only focused and participating in one life at a time. You can only ever physically feel the nerve endings in one body at a time—

where your consciousness is focused in that moment. In order to experience diverse patterns of life the soul must assume different physical bodies. A male body thriving on being a military commander cannot experience childbirth, so it would be necessary to have different lives to experience both. Reincarnation is the process of trying different roles in different bodies.

The soul goes through a series of lives to learn various lessons it wants to understand. You cannot be both a master and a slave in the same life, but you could in two different lives. You may want to accept the power and majesty of your soul essence while in physical form but be unable to fully appreciate the totality in just one lifetime. You would then have to try in a different body from a little different angle to see if you get it. Each of these factors requires your concentration in a new way.

You might argue that people can multitask; to a degree we agree. However, people cannot learn efficiently if they are just using a portion of their brain. If you are text messaging while walking, at some point you are going to walk into something or get yourself hurt. Both tasks would then be unfinished and would have to be redone to complete them.

Our soul essence is not restrained by a body or by the need to differentiate between lessons. For the soul, everything is happening simultaneously. But you can experience the full impact of only one act at a time—that upon which you focus. This is like a compact disc. It has many tracks upon it, each one a recording of an event. Can you read all of them at once? No! You have to focus on one track and then it is intelligible.

Life contracts

While still at Home, the soul makes a series of contracts concerning lessons that it wishes to experience in its coming lifetime. These will allow other souls, mostly soul mates from its closest soul group, to help it to be presented with situations that trigger lessons. Since most of the contracts are made with familiar souls, the very essence of them is familiar when you are both on Earth in human form.

You will also have occasion to meet souls from your group with whom you have not made contracts for this particular life. Even though you have no contract they will seem very well known to you because you have shared other lifetimes with them.

Karma

Our main message, taught through the *Masters of the Spirit World* books and blog, is that of reincarnation. A word we often use, which is sometimes misunderstood, is "karma."

Karma, as we use the word, does *not* mean retribution or punishment. Karma is the energy that radiates out from an event experienced by an individual. It is recorded in that soul's akashic record for future reference, but it does not predetermine future lives unless the soul itself makes the specific decision to make that energy a part of another incarnation. This decision can be either conscious or unconscious.

A conscious decision to have the energy from one life affect another may come, for example, if the soul has experienced causing someone to become a cripple and has watched the problems the person had. The soul might then choose to see how it would fare under the same circumstances and would plan this feature into its next life.

An unconscious decision could occur when a soul has previously decided upon a particular life lesson and then has not completed it during that life. It will then have the energy of that incomplete action still firing in its aura or energy field. This may cause a more difficult example of the same lesson to pop up in a subsequent life because it had not finished what it desired to accomplish. Even with the unconscious uncompleted activity in the background, the soul may choose to skip a lifetime before tackling it again. Freedom of choice, not karma or prior intentions, determines your next life.

It is possible for a soul to choose to spend a life as an animal. (Our channel has chosen to experience lives as a dolphin, a black panther, and an eagle.) It is not a very common occurrence to go inter-species, but some souls wish to have the abilities that only come with an animal existence. The decision is completely made with freedom of choice and has nothing to do with karma or behavior in a prior lifetime.

Spirit or soul?

The difference between "spirit" and "soul" is primarily a matter of semantics. The nuances of the English language, and the common interpretations placed upon certain words by different groups, are very confusing. For all practical purposes, spirit and soul are one and the same. Whenever one experiences something, the other shares in the benefits.

If you want to get down to specifics, soul is the term that has come to be associated with the essence of each being, the energy of Source that defines an individualized piece of Source. Spirit is a term that has become associated with the human consciousness of the soul. The soul is the unconscious state, or the repository of all the experience that has occurred outside the range of this incarnation's consciousness.

You can think of the soul as the internal organs of the human and the spirit as the skin that is visible to all. Whatever happens to the skin affects the health of the inside and vice versa. The soul is generally not visible to other humans unless they are very enlightened. The spirit of a person may be seen and felt by a majority of the population.

So what happens to these definitions when the soul leaves the body? If the person goes Home the consciousness is one and the same—soul and spirit. If the person has difficulty getting Home, the spirit remains cut off from knowledge of the soul and wanders around trying to contact people and other spirits to determine what has happened to it. Back at Home, awareness reunites them.

Life after death

Upon your Earth there has always been a fascination about life after death. The questions that you frequently ask of us are about those who have left body form and returned home: "Are they happy?" "Are they still mad at me?" "Will they forgive me?" "Are they getting what they justly deserve for what they did to me?" These questions basically come from a misunderstanding of what Home is like.

Unfortunately, there are still a lot of misconceptions. Once your soul leaves your physical shell, it has no touchable solid form unless you choose to use some of your energy to create a body. The bottom line, so to speak, is that as a soul you are nothing more than an amorphous [cloud-like] energetic mass. We are hearing some say "that's yucky!" In point of fact it allows one soul to join with the matrix of all that exists, and to know everything, and to be in more than one place at a time, because there are no restraints or restrictions placed upon it. This is the ultimate in freedom!

The questions we are most frequently asked come from the idea that your loved ones are just your loved ones. However, each soul has spent many different lifetimes with many different families and friends. The lifetime that you are aware of is one in which you made various contracts with the deceased person, before coming down, to have learning experiences.

35

Factors that create feelings of anger, regret, and hatred within you were all predetermined by you to provide you with lessons that you yourself sought. To the departed they are merely academic now. We carry no unresolved emotions into the unconditional love of Home—unless we choose to, if we will not let go of them.

Some discarnate souls separated from the physical body may still cling to that need to feel physical because they want to continue on with that past life. They are souls who have failed to complete at least one of the lessons they sought to learn. They want to go on and complete the work even though their body is no longer viable. They cling in physical desperation to that body which identifies who they think they are.

This occurs because they refuse to let go of the ego that defined who they were in the purely physical dimension. They still remain a slave to the thinking brain; they have not embraced their soul. With these ideas paramount, the soul-in-body remains connected to Earth and haunts or constantly contacts those who remain. Eventually, however, it will come to understand its situation and return Home.

The soul who has embraced its pure identity exists at Home in unconditional love, where there is no hate, no fear, no regret, no judgment. That soul is available, if not engaged in other pursuits, to communicate with those on Earth at its pleasure. It is totally purged of residual emotional issues stemming from interaction on Earth with other souls. So there is nothing to forgive, to make up for, nothing but love for all souls and all their journeys.

Responsibility

Responsibility is something that all humans say they want but few really want at all. Children can't wait to grow up, adolescents can't wait to get a driver's license, students can't wait to finish school, but then reality sinks in. When each phase of life is reached it comes with its own responsibilities. Children are no longer waited on hand and foot and have to face the consequences of their decisions. The driver must pay for fuel and insurance and obey a book full of laws in order to drive. Once school is over, the search for employment begins, and then the day-to-day grind of being under someone's thumb starts.

Responsibility is totally assuming consequences for each and every choice you make in life. For most people it is unthinkable to seek such a task. It is so much better to allow someone else to make decisions for you, because then when things don't turn out the way you want, it is not your fault but rather theirs.

Choosing to give your choices to another is allowing them to have power over you—almost like saying that you trust them to make better decisions than you could because they know more about you than you do yourself. It's kind of a crazy proposition, but a seemingly safe one when you don't want to regret what you have done. The problem is that you never grow in understanding life or the lessons you came here to experience. You are just a game piece on the board of life instead of being the player directing the pieces. When are you ready to call the shots? Whenever you start gathering the facts about a situation and making the decisions all on your own. It can be at any stage in the human process that you have enough confidence to make the choices. Sometimes a soul never reaches this stage in a lifetime.

Souls and gender

Do souls have a sexually significant gender? That is: are they either male or female, a male/female hybrid, or sexless? The answer is no. What you understand as a person's sex is part of the duality of planet Earth. Outside of the dimension of

Earth there is no duality—no opposites, so therefore no sexual differences. A soul has all the characteristics that are considered to be emotionally male or female on Earth, all in one package.

When humans channel, they can only interpret the vibrational information they receive in terms of their own human experience. If they have never before been exposed to the understanding that an entity such as a soul does not need to have a gender, they may feel obligated to assign one anyway. This is because, in their knowledge base, all beings have a sexual orientation.

Since a soul has all of that which you consider to be the characteristics of both sexes together in a single container, the energetic feelings of any portion of that container are both male and female. If channels access the female energy they will think you are female. If they access the male energy they will swear you are male—yet you are energetically both. You have chosen to spend this experience in a female body. At Home, you are a soul without a specific sexual designation but with all of the feelings that enable you to play either role, as you choose, whenever you come to Earth.

Indigo and crystal children

Advanced souls, called "indigos" and "crystals," are coming down to the planet at this time to help out with the chaos that is going on. Both groups of youngsters are advanced souls who have incarnated but do not have complete amnesia as to the former lives they have lived on planet Earth. Therefore they seem like adults in children's bodies.

The indigos are very psychic and are geared toward leadership, so they do not like to take orders. They have been dubbed "rule busters" by many educational groups. They have very inquisitive minds and are easily bored, because learning comes easily for them since they still remember having done the same things before. They do not spend time on things that they have already mastered, so they are frequently thought to have ADD or ADHD.* It is important to stimulate them continually until they find their little niche—then they will pull themselves along like prodigies.

Crystal children are empathic but more introspective. They have some residual memories of other lives as well. They cannot stand conflict and have been called peacemakers within society. They must have time alone to balance themselves and are very connected to the energy of the Earth. They sometimes just want to go inside and run away from the conflicts, so they may be diagnosed as autistic or may become depressed. Give them a lot of love but also their space.

* ADD stands for Attention Deficit Disorder, and ADHD for Attention Deficit Hyperactivity Disorder.

Is romance necessary?

Souls come into body to be able to experience a number of different feelings and lessons. Romantic love, the love shared between two human beings, can only be felt with the nervous system of the physical body. Souls cannot feel a romantic type of love. However, they can certainly detect an all-consuming unconditional love, like that of which they are composed when in energetic form.

Some souls come down with a lesson of experiencing all aspects of physical romantic love. The ups and downs of the emotions, the give and take between two people who may be totally different, the sense of abandonment or betrayal that is strongest when associated with romantic love: these can only be felt with a human body.

Society tells everyone that the family is the most important aspect of life. This provides more people in the form of children and creates less discord created by love triangles, stalking, and jealousies. Society is ego-driven and judges right or wrong and compliance with everyone else in the group. Love for another human is encouraged and accepted. Love for oneself is considered narcissistic and selfish.

On the spiritual soul level, after the lessons are completed, the soul finds its path back to Home by following the unconditional love that is contained within. But even before that, souls can truly love another only to the extent that they love themselves. Without a sense of self-love, the person has no idea what love feels like and therefore cannot understand love for someone else. Each soul needs to have a combination of spiritual unconditional love and romantic love to experience incarnate life to the fullest.

Chapter Three
Belief Systems

The word "belief" suggests the idea of a religious faith or philosophy. The Masters do not promote this idea but look instead to individuals attempting to know themselves, free from the edicts and belief systems in which they may have become confined as children. They look at faith and truth in a way that may seem disturbing—because we are being asked to think things out for ourselves.

Belief systems
Source
What kind of faith?
Scripture and spirituality
Finding the way
What feels right to you?
Loving oneself
Is there one true religion?
Fear
Truth
Only one life
Am I on the right path?
There are no absolutes
Destiny
Creating hell
Death, hell, and God

Belief Systems

Once people develop belief systems, since they mostly come from parents, relatives, society, religious groups, and peers, it is very difficult to get them to realize that they have the ability to change them. Just as with the hard-drive memory of a computer, your belief systems keep controlling every aspect of your life until they are deleted, overwritten, or rewritten.

Most people are even unaware of the beliefs that control them so completely. If you ask why they have done something, frequently their answer is that they have always done it a certain way, or that is the way that everyone does it. If you press them further for a reason, they simply cannot tell you why.

The first step in getting people to analyze their behavior is to keep asking the "why" question. Pin them down. Don't let them avoid thinking about their reasons. When they begin to question themselves, that is when they see that they never thought about their actions, which are just automatic. When you get them to this point, suggest that they start to watch their own behavior and see if they have a good reason for doing what they do.

Source

When it comes to a belief in God you first have to define how you feel about "God." Do you still accept that it is some benevolent being that sits in judgment over all that you do? Or do you feel that judgment is just a human quality that only facilitates learning life lessons? Once a precise formula has been thrown out you must invent or accept another.

We will tell you what we know about the energy that you call "God," which we generally refer to as "Source." Source is an energy composed of unconditional love. It existed before all else and encompassed everything that was. Source wished to have a way to better understand the magnificence of unconditional love, so it broke off fractions of itself to have varying experiences with and without love. These fractions we call souls.

Since each soul is a little piece of the Source, it can exhibit the same qualities of Source, if it chooses. Therefore, for your purposes, you contain within you a fraction of Source, or as you call it, God. When you "lose your faith in God" you have lost your faith in yourself.

Most people abandon their faith in themselves because they do not want to have to assume responsibility for their actions and the lessons they are experiencing. Because of who you are (and everyone else in creation is), to find your answers you simply have to go within and accept the feelings that you find there. Those feelings are the essence of you as a soul—as a part of Source.

Arguing, condemning, or ridiculing behavior will only force it deeper into the person's psyche. As your friends try to find reasons for their actions, they will have flashbacks to their youth and will see that what they did then makes absolutely no sense now. It is like old, outdated information that has to be recognized as such to be purged from our memory.

They must accept that the past is past and the present is now—a new blank slate over which they have control. They may be ready to see belief systems as limiting their horizon by keeping them stuck in the past, or they may very well be so comfortable there that they don't want to move along. Freedom of choice rules.

What kind of faith?

All your Earth religions teach that faith is an important aspect of their dogma. The faith they implore you to have may be in Allah, God, Ishvara, Jehovah, or Shakti. We ask that

43

you maintain your faith, but in the person who is significant in this current life experience—yourself!

It is a very common excuse in society to expect other sources to be responsible for what is happening to you in your life. Why not blame an outside power for all the uncomfortable situations in which you find yourself involved? If you insist on outside control, you never have to take responsibility or chastise yourself for anything. But you cannot learn about your life lessons if you never evaluate how you have handled them and the decisions arising from your freedom of choice.

If you have faith in yourself and your soul's pathway, you will learn from each experience you have because you admit that you have created your own reality by the choices you have made. Faith also allows you to have the confidence in each step you take, each decision or choice directing you to the fastest way to complete your lessons so that you may move toward your ultimate goal.

Take back that power which is your life and your right, and maintain the faith that is yours alone. Enjoy the choices dictated by that faith, and live a fruitful life on the Earth.

Scripture and spirituality

Various versions of the Christian Bible were compiled during a period of time when most people were illiterate and needed stories in order for them to learn and understand. The rulers and church hierarchy provided all the educational opportunities for the peasants. As well as teaching them, they established strict belief systems as a means of exercising control over the people. The educated hesitated to give too much hope or knowledge to the uneducated lest they rebel and go elsewhere for learning or salvation.

Through the centuries the recorded verses went thus: First, they were written in a manner that made the people fear the wrath of God as personified by the clergy; then, the God-force had to be recognized as outside of and superior to the physical; finally, a reward system had to be set up— heaven—so that following the mandates of "God," or, rather, the clergy, would bring rewards after life on Earth.

Scriptural interpretation changed very little as literacy became more common. Bible study continued to teach that a reward system existed among humans, and that God is outside of us and superior to us. Most modern biblical interpretations presented in classes adhere to these principles. Most Bible teachers still believe that the Bible is to be accepted as the Word of God without question, and that it has nothing to do with how it feels or resonates with you.

To change thoroughly entrenched belief it is necessary to present ideas that modify that belief. Then you must offer an alternative interpretation and get inquisitive people to think and feel for themselves.

Without these steps, people do not know that they have a choice of beliefs, so they accept the original teaching without question. Once it is realized that other interpretations may be made, people can use their freedom of choice to determine whatever belief feels right to them. In all things we want you to know that you have freedom of choice. We wanted to go into this area, which was previously viewed as sacred, to let you know there are choices of belief here as well.

We encourage you to read the Bible with an open heart and mind. Feel what the verses say to you; do not accept standard interpretations blindly, but if they resonate with you, by all means hold them dear. Review also the possibility of a different perspective and see how that feels. Honor yourself!

Finding the way

Some of you have found or have been led to information that is a key to your continued enlightenment. For you to integrate and live within these feelings you must accept them as your own and tell other people about them. This is very difficult to do, unless you are with like-minded individuals, and especially if your new principles conflict with belief systems that have defined your world up to this point.

May we suggest that the first step is to find a group that believes as you do or feels as you feel. If our words resonate with you, you may feel at home in groups that follow these tenets. It is also important for you to experience mind/body practices that make you aware of the energies within your body. They include meditation, yoga, and tai chi, which may give you a sense of certainty about your new path.

What we find crucial to total personal integration is that you *hear* yourself "lay claim" to your new beliefs. These may include that you are made in the image and likeness of the Source, and that you were broken off from Source and therefore have the power to intentionally manifest the things that you desire. By laying claim to beliefs, we mean that until you tell others what it is you now believe, you will not feel comfortable existing simultaneously in two different worlds, the old and the new.

People may say they cannot do that. The ego within the human mind controls conscious activity very powerfully. Childhood beliefs and the teaching of others, which you have readily accepted, act as default settings. They are superimposed on all new ideas by your ego until you overwrite those beliefs by actually speaking your new truths to yourself and others. Until you feel comfortable admitting to yourself how you now see yourself, try keeping a journal acknowledging your acceptance of these new

46

principles. It will start the process of moving to your new way of thinking and living. May your journey be comfortable.

What feels right to you?

We do not wish to get into a discussion about belief systems concerning and contained within organized religions. The teachings of each individual religion and sect are for each member to interpret individually or even choose to follow blindly. No one from this side of the veil [the "Other Side" or "Home"] will *ever* tell you what to think or not to think.

The whole premise for life on planet Earth is to feel what is right for you and to exercise your freedom of choice to determine what you will accept and live as a belief system or reality. Part of all freedom-of-choice selections (made while in human form) is accepting responsibility for your own decisions. It is impossible to learn anything if you do only what you are told instead of having to experiment on your own to see what feels right to you.

Don't be concerned about what other people are doing. The choices that are right for them may not feel right to you. Many of you repeatedly worry about who you are within your environment. You have many abilities and talents but don't have the faith or confidence in yourself to pursue one with all your energy. Worrying about what the rest of the world thinks about you, or if you meet their expectations, derails your fledgling attempts at getting comfortable with an identity and choices that help create it.

To aid your search, we ask, "Just who are you?" Are you a soul on a journey of self-discovery? Or are you a human who must please other humans? Both are paths that will take you through this adventure you are having in your present body. Neither is right or wrong. They are simply different ways to live—the choice is yours alone. Don't let the decision take all your effort.

If you wish to please those around you, listen to what they say and sometimes demand, and mold your behavior to the belief systems they impose. If you are at a point to establish your own Earthly soul journey, take the proffered information from others and then feel if it resonates within you. If it does, follow it. If it does not, reach inside to find the vibration that motivates movement for you. Define the identity you choose to live.

Loving oneself

Have you ever been in a room and a very spiritual person enters while you have your back to the door? Is it not possible to feel a change in the atmosphere in the room such as a new sense of peace, tranquility, and stability enveloping you? Or, conversely, when a very angry person enters behind you, won't you feel a sense of fear, dread, or despair? These experiences all occur when energy variations disrupt the atmosphere.

All souls (and therefore bodies they inhabit) are sensitive to the vibrations of other energies around them. When you see something beautiful don't you watch it, as long as it is in sight, to capture some of that beauty to take with you?

True self-love is tapping into the soul of oneself to touch the unconditional love that is the essence of all of us. As souls, we are all unconditional love. That love requires nothing, including another person, for us to be able to bathe in its warmth.

Loving your self is the ability to go inside and touch that unconditional love. In order to reach that state of awareness, you must love every aspect of where you are within your present physical being.

You may say: I am fat or ugly, I have a lousy job or am a drunk; how can I love myself? Our answer is that all we are asking you to do is to love is your essence—the unconditional love of your soul. You don't even have to *like* everything about the body you currently call home, but you need to love who you are as a soul. You have the ability to change the body that encompasses your soul, unless that is part of this life's lesson.

The love you seek, even crave from others, is reflected from you. You can love another only to the extent that you love yourself. If you hate yourself, you are incapable of truly loving another because you do not feel that you are worthy of their love.

When you love everything about the beauty of your soul, you know that you are as good as everyone else and worthy of receiving their love. There are no fears that can exist in such an environment, and therefore you are only aware of the essence—the love.

Is there one true religion?

A religion is a set of beliefs on which one fashions one's existence. It is a set of rituals, prayers, activities, and customs that regulate every aspect of being. These are dictated to everyone by an individual or a hierarchy within the belief system. Their guarantee to those who adhere to all the rules and regulations is of various benefits for this physical life and beyond, regardless of the adherents' reasons for coming to human form.

All incarnates come to the Earth to learn lessons through experiences. They learn these lesson through using their freedom of choice to find what resonates with their soul and what moves them from negative energies into positive ones. One of the ways this may occur is to choose to follow a particular religion because it resonates with your humanity, and you sense changes taking place in your understanding and awareness of your soul's path. This is enlightenment.

Before we go any further let us ask this question: Is there a particular language upon your planet that if spoken by all would ensure peace? Are there not armed conflicts all over the world between peoples who all call a single language their own? What of the factions within a society that resist being grouped together with one holding opposing views to those of their peers? Is not each and every human soul on an individual journey? Is one method any better than any other?

Just as no universal language will suffice for your diversified planet, one belief system cannot be the answer to all souls' journeys. While all souls were identical as they came from Source, no two physical incarnations are the same. The knowledge of each soul is the knowledge of all while in spirit form, because we are all interconnected; so each soul chooses its own direction and lessons. The process of learning is not to repeat what others have done unless you crave the same experience since you already know how it turns out.

Fear

There are only two energies in the world: love and fear. If you don't love something, some aspect of fear will arrive to drive you away from any contact with it. You have the belief system fear and the "I don't love myself" layer of fear.

To rid yourself of the belief systems you must ask yourself, every time a fear appears, why do I feel this way? If you are truthful you will be able to go back to the time that the belief was written into your brain. You then have the freedom of choice to keep it around or delete it from your life.

The fear of death and of spirits or ghosts reflects your upbringing and the views of society, which have stuck with you both consciously and unconsciously. We call them belief systems. Most of the time you are unaware you are being affected by these rigid rules, even though they shape your life. Organized religions and society work on a basis of reward and punishment. If you don't do what they tell you, you will be punished. In religion it may be by going to hell. You start to fear death because you believe you will be judged by someone else's standards, so you feel the result is out of your hands.

Religions, and some societies too, feel that ghostly spirits are bad people who are caught in between Earth and hell, and should be avoided at all costs. You are threatened from an early age that the boogie man will get you if you are not good. You are told there are demons under your bed and in the closet—so go to bed and stay there. Is it any wonder that you have these fears?

To find peace, examine your fears. Take each thing, meditate upon it, and see what feelings come from inside of you. What do you associate with these thoughts? Then if you can put someone else's face to the fear, give it back to that person and form your own opinions.

Acceptance of the presence of the unconditional love that is your soul allows you to love yourself and everything you are experiencing. When you know you are eternal and can feel the love of the universe, nothing can hurt you or make you afraid. When you think you are alone, everything is scary. Connect with yourself and banish the fear.

You are a soul who came from Source, and returning is called "going Home." You don't need to fear returning to Source, to your true essence. When you are between lives on Earth, you are in spirit form and wander around observing things. Do not fear your fellow souls.

Truth

What is truth? Truth varies with the individual and may change from time to time even within each person. Truth is a combination of what you see, hear, feel, need, and accept. Initially, you are set up for your truth by parents, teachers, and all whom you see as authority figures. They provide the truths, or belief systems, by which you lead your life. Then, when you finally realize you have total freedom of choice as to what you accept into your life, you choose your own truth independent of outside influence.

To reach your own truth and to feel comfortable with it, you should take all of the information that feels right to you, spend some time with it, and then adopt that which completely resonates with you. Do not feel bad if, at some point in the future, the truth you have accepted suddenly no longer serves you. Thank the energies and send them on their way, while you find a concept that now resonates within you.

The universal truth is that the soul never ceases its existence. It is immortal and chooses to have varied experiences, which it accomplishes by coming to Earth in a number of scenarios. Within each life it encases itself in a physical form that allows it to interact with other souls similarly attired. When the soul finishes an experience, it returns Home to its completely energetic state to plan for its next adventure in physicality and learning. Each one of these roles begins with a birth and ends with a death, but these affect only the body that has been adopted, not the soul itself. When you are engaged in one of these lives, you are always exactly where you have chosen to be when you are there. As long as the soul is aware of its surroundings, and not running away from them, it is achieving the knowledge it incarnated to experience.

A truth, within the human psyche, is something that souls accept as applying to them at that moment in time. It is relevant to them alone since they set the parameters of desires, needs, experience, and lessons. For a single lifetime the truths for the soul may change a number of times. In first grade, your truth is that you cannot do algebra; in 10th grade, that you cannot do calculus; and in 12th grade, that you are not a licensed physician. Are you seeing that the pattern has a lot to do with experience as well as belief? The human ego makes judgments about truth and what is right and wrong. In the spiritual non-physical world there is no right and wrong, so there are no absolutes.

A soul that knows its nature is an extremely powerful energy and can create whatever it needs to experience. If souls come to Earth to experience cancer and to succumb to it, no amount of chemotherapy or anything else is going to cure it. If a soul did not plan to die by poison, then consuming a poison might sicken it, but would not kill the body. If people's faith is strong enough and it is part of their journey, even caustic substances will have no effect.

The universe has no truths because it has no judgment declaring that only one thing is correct. Since each soul is on its own unique journey, we say there are no absolutes controlling factors within that life. The closest we can come to a certain fact, which some may say is absolute, is that all souls are a part of Source coming from unconditional love, and to that love they shall eventually return.

Only one life

Within some belief systems there is confusion concerning the number of lifetimes that a soul may experience. There is a segment of the human population that believes the only physical existence that a soul has is the very one it is undergoing at the time the question is asked. Most of these are followers of an organized religion that is based upon a system of reward and punishment—the end result of a life being a glorious ascent into heaven or an ignominious descent into hell.

Another segment follows a belief system where the soul enters a series of lives dictated by the bad karma it earns in one lifetime and must work off in others. This continues until a state of enlightenment has been reached, at which time the soul may return Home. Some feel there are a certain number of lives, rather like the proverbial nine lives of the cat, that they must endure before they can return Home.

Each soul does have only one life—a life in which it takes on human form over and over again to confront many different types of experiences. The number of experiences—"lives" as human beings call them—is completely a matter of choice for each soul. It may choose to have a hundred or only twenty-five; it depends on how many Earth life lessons it wants to complete. There are absolutely no requirements.

The right path

We wish to address a frequently asked question: "How do I know that what I am doing in this life is what I am supposed to be doing?"

As human beings it is very common for you to need validation of your actions and decisions. As you entered life upon the Earth plane, you began each new chapter by deciding in advance the specific lessons you wished to make a part of your soul's wisdom. You planned the particulars of some of the lessons, though with others you just had a general idea of what you sought to accomplish. Once you entered the physical structure of each body you inhabited, however, you always did so with no memory of any of these prior decisions.

Initially, your physical body is helped by being raised within an array of belief systems contributed by parents, teachers, society, and religions. The purpose of these belief systems is to define for you how other people feel you should behave and what they feel you should believe.

A parallel illustration of this idea is the operating system running the program on which this message has been recorded. A programmer wrote the program to do a multitude of tasks and to prevent certain functions from occurring. If you do not assess the correctness for you of these functions, you blindly adhere to the programming without question, and may well discover that you are unable to carry out certain of the plans you formulated. It is the same in your physical life. By failing to question why you cannot do what you have envisioned, you are giving away to other people your power to determine your direction in life.

If you merely intellectualize the decisions and directions you take—using only your brain—you will accept the beliefs and directions imbedded in you by others. All the information within your brain comes from outside of your self. It is implanted within you by the words of others, either told to you orally or read by you visually. You are completely cut out of the decision process as you follow along like a little lemming.

The belief systems that have been your guide for a large portion of your life are not permanent and immovable. You may remove them from impacting your thinking by taking each statement in turn and *feeling* if it represents the right path for you.

If you believe the idea your teacher put into your head when calling you "stupid," then identify with it and let it direct your life. But if, instead, you know that you are not stupid (because of everything you have been able to accomplish successfully within your life), then erase all trace of that negative energy from your memory and rewrite your mental program to say that you are a brilliant physicist (or whatever else you may have become).

There is another aspect of this physical experience that most people ignore. You are aware of feelings or intuition coming from the knowledge and wisdom of your soul. If, whenever you have an important decision to make, you say, "What do I think?" you give the power to others. But if, instead, you say, "What do I feel?" you are searching inside for your own inner knowledge and wisdom, and you are taking responsibility for your own decisions. This is the only way that you can truly learn your lessons. It's the same if you only watch sports on television and never participate in them yourself—you will never have the experience of the exertion and the elation of that accomplishment.

Responding again to that question we began with, "How do I know that what I am doing in this life is what I am supposed to be doing?" we have two questions for you: "Are you listening to your intuition and feeling what you want to do?" and "Do you feel that what you are doing is what you should be doing?"

These are really just rhetorical questions because now we have a statement of universal wisdom to give you. It is: "Your soul ensures that you always do exactly the right thing at the right time to gain the experience that you sought to have."

Take the time to laugh at yourself for all the choices you can't now remember making—while you enjoy this wonderful journey of unique experiences.

There are no absolutes

Belief systems are the rules and regulations that we consciously and unconsciously adhere to, because we have been trained to accept them. Most of them we follow unconsciously because we do not know how impactful they are upon our lives, or we haven't identified their effect upon us. When we "see" them for the first time, they become conscious, and we then make the decision either to change them or continue to follow them. These are mostly behavioral.

Then there are purely scientific things—such as the weight of an object, the temperature at which it melts, burns, or freezes—which are fairly constant or universally absolute. These are the solids, gases, minerals, and chemicals in their pure, unadulterated and uncombined forms. But even these factors are affected by humidity, altitude, temperature, and size of sample. To approach an absolute you have to be able to reproduce <u>exactly</u> every minute factor involved.

Once you start talking about physical beings, all bets are off as far as finding an absolute is concerned. No two human beings are identical, even identical twins once they are born and start living separate lives. Three factors influence the type of results: First, how is the physical organism functioning? Second, do you realize you have the ability to manifest influences on your physical body? And, third, is there any lesson you agreed to experience that will affect numbers one or two?

If your body has absorbed toxic substances, it has toxic substances. If there is no lesson involved can you rid yourself of the toxins? Yes! Can you live with them and not get sick if you believe you will not get sick and don't need to learn differently? Yes! Are the toxins not there just because you don't know they are there? No!

So, when we say there are no absolutes, we are referring to the journey of the soul on the mental, emotional, physical, and metaphysical planes.

Destiny

Destiny is a concept that only has importance to those people within the physical realm who believe they have no freedom of choice. To accept you have a specific destiny, you say that everything about your life is predestined (predetermined or decided), and it will happen as it has been written (by whom they never say!), and you can't do a thing about it.

Many societies, nationalities, and religious organizations have belief systems that accept the determination of a destiny. Controlling bodies would like all people to think that they are destined to do this or that—then the organization comes in and moderates what the path of destiny consists of and how they can help with the decided tasks. This generally accomplishes whatever the group wishes to see done.

Accept and believe you have the freedom of choice to determine everything in your life and you will always decide your own fate.

Many times we have spoken on the purpose of each soul. It is to come to Earth with various lessons it wishes to understand. In learning its lessons the soul may then truly know its own nature. The nature of the soul is unconditional love. To be happy and motivated, work toward always feeling love. Accept everything about yourself at every stage of your life, even the things you don't understand or like. Those things signal to you what to work on to feel your love.

Creating hell

The transitional point is that the soul, upon leaving the body it has used in a lifetime, doesn't go immediately Home unless it makes the effort to do so. The entire transition from human being to essential soul is transacted by the decision and with the intention of the soul itself. Being more in the physical realm at the start of this phase, the thought process of the human ego is still firing away with its "knowledge" of the way things "should be."

If the soul has accepted a portion of society's belief that the death process brings it into a period of judgment for everything it has done during the physical life, it will expect to be judged and punished for its transgressions. If it believes it has sinned and merits punishment, it may expect a place or condition it has been told is hell. The soul then creates that place with its powerful intention so that it may move into that next segment of its existence. At that point, the soul is so convinced this is its only possible step that it does not realize it has the freedom of choice to go straight into unconditional love.

If the soul knows it is leaving all judgment behind and going into the area of unconditional love, it can allow itself to feel that unconditional love, immediately bypassing any need for the expected pearly gates and judgment scenario. Even if the soul has created a hell for itself, its guides will stay close and look for any opening in which it asks for assistance, which generally comes when it is frustrated by nothing occurring but the fire and brimstone it has envisioned. The guides will then be there to offer help to the soul to find its way to the unconditional love of the non-judgmental space of soul existence (Home). This can be done, however, only when the soul releases its creation of judgment—its own vision of hell.

Death, hell, and God

By religious definition hell is definitely not a place for rest and relaxation. But is there a place called hell? No. Is the description of hell synonymous with a condition wherein a soul feels tormented and inconsolable? Absolutely! And where such a place exists is none other than the planet under your feet!

Earth is a place of duality, where everything has a polar opposite. For every fantastically marvelous feeling there is an equally strong negative feeling of devastation and suffering. Once the soul leaves its body here (or, in other words, dies), it leaves this negative space and enters a place of unconditional love where no negativity exists. A soul may experience what has been referred to as hell while living on Earth, but once it leaves Earth it has a place (that some call "heaven") where judgment does not exist and where everything is unconditional love.

The term "God" has become associated with the image of a man dressed all in white with long hair and a beard who is the arbiter of judgment for all souls. Judgment can only exist in a place where there is right and wrong or positive and negative. Since those conditions only exist on planet Earth, a god could only exist there.

Is there a single divine entity? No. Is there a force in the universe that is omnipotent? Yes. This is the universal energy that encompasses all that is. You and all individual souls broke off from this energy, remain a part of it, commune with it, and re-unite with it when desired. This can occur at any time the soul is not contained in a body shell.

Chapter Four
Enlightenment

We must look within to discover true harmony between our eternal soul and our temporal body and mind. With help from meditation and other disciplines, we discover our self and how we may enjoy this new awareness. When we truly understand who we are, the working together of our mind and soul becomes a dynamic relationship.

Your essence
Change your reality
Love and peace on Earth
Walking meditation
Listen to the music
Negativity
Where has all the love gone?
Intentional creativity
Free will or predestination?
Cut off from spirit
Awakening the kundalini
The ascension process

Your Essence

Let us take a look at your essence: it is a non-physical energy being that can be connected to everything at once. Your core, the soul, is a piece of the Source, and therefore it is omniscient, omnipresent, and omnificent [unlimited in creative power]. It may choose to have its consciousness in one place at a time or in more than one place. Understanding the frailty of the human shell as a container, with all the things that can affect and afflict it, would it be your optimal choice for experiencing, say, a worry-free vacation?

The human body is perfect in all its imperfections for the life lessons you come to experience within a duality-based planet. Planet Earth is currently the only place set up for the soul to immerse itself in polar opposites—for the purpose of knowing the greatness of unconditional love, and through that experience, the magnificence of Source.

Contrary to what a majority of the inhabitants of planet Earth believe, you are not alone in your solar system. It is very presumptuous of human beings to think that they are the ultimate in intelligence, self-awareness, and adaptability. Your scientists believe your evolutionary process is the only pattern for a species to undertake. They further believe that no other circumstances can sustain an existence as great and grand as yours.

Other places for interacting with souls on a non-totally energetic basis do not require a body that will allow you to feel sadness, anger, fear, betrayal, or any other duality lesson. So if your soul wants to study communication through various types of vocalization, all it needs is some type of vibratory flap that it can control to experiment with variations. Or if your soul wants to engage in historical remembrances and debates concerning cosmology, all it needs is the ability to share ideas with another soul—no body, no mouth, just thoughts!

You cannot identify an energetic being that doesn't have a form you recognize. An example would be that sometimes other beings watch planet Earth, out of curiosity, camouflaged as a cloud. Would you see them as anything other than a cloud? Just as you cannot compare an apple to an orange, you cannot compare a human to those of other compositions.

Change your reality

Our comment is about your ability to create the physical perception of your soul's Earthly existence. Many of you are unaware that you have this capability. For many more it is an elusive dream that you yearn to make real. In order to power this inner capacity to fine-tune your understanding, you need only tap into your divinity. No, the concept of divinity is not heresy; rather, it is a statement of fact that defines you as an individual piece of Source.

Each soul was broken off from Source in order to learn lessons and to gain wisdom. Every one of you is of the same energy, with the same abilities, as Source. Before you ever began this particular experience on Earth you decided what lessons you wanted to learn, and chose the basic requirements for putting yourself into a situation where it would be easy to have the experiences you desired.

Now, while you are in physical form, you may have a "do-as-I-do" mentality that makes you want to comply with the rules of the immediate surrounding society. The belief systems you adopt from those around you can help you make choices that allow you to learn lessons, but they also can be used as a box within which you choose to spend your time on Earth following the whim of others.

You really do have an alternative. You may tap into your inner power, realizing and acknowledging that this life is an illusion you have created around you. With this realization, you may choose to create a new reality that is all your own, to enable you to become more aware both of the lessons you came to learn and of your true essence as a soul. Each soul's reality is what it experiences at any given time, and it changes as its perspective changes.

Some of you are asking yourselves right now, "What the 'bleep' are they talking about?" The fact we are referring to is that, when you have a certainty about your life (something that you have convinced yourself exists), that is all you can see.

So, for example, if you deny that non-physical beings and energies exist, you will never be able to interact with us on your own. If you believe that you have no control over the way other people treat you, you simply will not. Again, if you believe that you will contract a certain ailment because "everyone" gets it, then you surely will.

Simply put, your conscious mind is very powerful, and what you accept as reality will become your reality. So how do you change your reality? Count the following pointers off on your fingers:

> **Accept** that you can change your reality.
> **Have faith** in your own abilities and who you truly are.
> **Believe** that you can accomplish what you desire.
> **Know** that you have all the power and ability to change.
> **Become** what you have accepted and believed in—knowing that you can transform your present experience.

So, how do you begin? Remember the phrase "Fake it until you make it"? Start by acting as if you are what you know you can become. It will not automatically come to you. Start slowly at first, banishing all negative thoughts whenever they pop into your conscious mind. Whenever they arrive, think instead of the happiest time in your life. When someone asks you how you are, always respond with a cheerful "fantastic" or "marvelous" or "never better" and soon that will become exactly how you feel. Live your life as a magnet for how you want your reality to become.

Love and peace on Earth

Souls all come from an origin of unconditional love, and when not having a physical experience, they exist in unconditional love. Were all incarnating souls to have only the memory of living in an aura of unconditional love, they would not be able to have any experience of things that are not love. Fear, hate, despair, loneliness, betrayal, brutality— all the lessons you choose to come to Earth to experience would then be beyond your reach and comprehension.

People speak of an ideal world for life on Earth, but why even come here if all you want is love? The answer is that you have such strong feelings about love because one of your life lessons is to find that love within yourself. So now you are projecting your need on those around you. You fear that you cannot have the love you crave unless the whole world also has such love.

If you reach deep inside yourself and connect with the divinity within you, which is your soul, you will bathe yourself in unconditional love. Then, not only will you stop projecting your needs onto others, but you will radiate that sensation of love so that others will seek their true selves as well. Go, now, and complete your mission with love.

Walking meditation

The goal or purpose of meditation is to be able to go within to connect with the energy of your essential soul. This may only be accomplished in quiet solitude. In today's world the noisiest distraction to contemplation is your over-active brain.

Schools of meditation teach you to begin by concentrating on your breathing, saying a mantra, or thinking about something that causes you to forget all else. All of these tricks work to divert your mind away from everyday thinking. But then you may find yourself fixating upon them.

Walking is another method of quieting the mind. At first you are concerned with where you are going, that you are not going to trip, and what the weather is like. With the monotony of the repeated steps, you get into a comfortable pattern that quiets your mind and allows you to hear your inner self.

You will also find an added benefit—the exercise. Physical exertion prevents you from folding up into a ball and impeding the free flow of energy throughout your body. As the body moves you become aware of the need to breathe deeply, bringing in and connecting to the energies of Mother Earth and Father Sky.

Another form of non-sitting meditation is moving meditation. This is normally done to the beat of music. Just allowing your body to respond to the vibration of the rhythm allows you again to tap into the inner workings of your physical self and feel your connection to the universe.

Listen to the music

We recognize that a lot of you are missing out on one of the ways that you can listen to us and connect to your soul. The vibrational means that we use to communicate with each other and to share in the unconditional love translates on your planet into what you call music. We can see a ton of blank stares right now. We are not being facetious.

Can you truly say that you have never been moved to tears, fear, or elation by the sound of music? Have you ever wondered why movies have an audio soundtrack embedded in them? Think of that music the next time you see a love story, a drama, or a horror film. The music talks to you with vibrations, or subliminally gets you "in the mood," as they say.

To start to hear us, practice by listening to nature. The sound of the wind and rain, the birds, the rustle of leaves, the call of an animal, all tell their unique stories to you. When you can hear the wind, listen to the music of our vibrational voice.

Negativity

We have received a lot of comments from people that they are unable to create what they want and need. The statements go something like this: "I've been trying..." "As hard and as much as I try..." "After I have succeeded in creating things, I think it is just dumb luck and then everything else fails."

What we are hearing in all these remarks is negativity and a total lack of confidence in your own power. You are erecting a brick wall of limitations. Words are magical in your physical dimension. What you say is what your consciousness and unconsciousness believes to be the truth. When you use an expression that indicates a lack of confidence in the outcome, such as "try" instead of "do," you are saying "I am not confident that I can complete this," which translates into "Here goes another failure"... and so it fails.

Why should you feel that you are worthy enough and good enough to create your own reality? You were broken off from the Source of all things. You have the same powers as Source to manifest for your needs. It is solely your conscious, human-empowered limitations that prevent you from being magnificent.

When you have cut loose all the human doubts and begin to have faith in yourself, you will find it easy to create, from your core power (your identity as a piece of Source), everything that you need. Getting back to core power, while in physical form, is one of the life lessons souls come to Earth to learn. Have faith in yourself. Be true to yourself. Honor yourself. Shed the negativity and live in love, light, and laughter.

Where has all the love gone?

Love is everywhere; you just have to allow yourself to see and feel it. As a child you lived in the moment in your own world, blocking out negativity, so that it was easy to receive and feel the love. As you got older you became concerned with the world around you as you related to others.

You identify with all the titles you have earned. With each of these identities came an individualized set of responsibilities that you assumed. You are barely able to peek over the top of your self-accepted requirements. They are barricades that prevent you from feeling the love outside of you.

What catches your attention now is the sensationalism of all the headlines relating to atrocities throughout the world. Your reaction to this negativity is to pull your head into your shell and peer skeptically at your surroundings. Those around you feel the fear and magnify it so that it reinforces your own feelings of the lack of love.

There are only two emotions in your world: love and fear. They are polar opposites, and one cannot exist in the presence of the other. Anything that you do not love, you fear in one form or another, be it hate, jealousy, revenge, or plain mind-numbing terror. Many souls come down to planet Earth to experience the battle between love and fear as a life lesson.

To return to the feeling of love you must let go of fear. You must examine in your life anything that is not love and see what lesson it is trying to teach you, so that you may learn it and move back to love. Inside each human shell is a magnificent, all-loving soul who gets buried in life lessons. Dig yours out and relish the unconditional love of the universe.

Intentional creativity

You constantly think about what you want to accomplish, but you don't put much energy into your intention to manifest that objective. Intention is the action caused by gathering all your energy, and the universal energy that you can take in, and funneling it into a manifestation of what it is that you desire. You are thereby creating the reality that you seek.

A number of people reading some of the current popular books believe that manifestation is an easy process. Simply take a picture of yourself as a doctor and you will materialize that result sometime in the future. Believe us, that will not just happen. If you do nothing to begin the process, you will have a nice picture and that is all.

Most people do not look upon intention as an action. They see it merely as something that they think about and wish for. You can spend all of the time in your world thinking about becoming a doctor, but until you perform the action of applying to medical school, taking the classes, and completing the internship, you have no way to become a doctor.

Part of the intention process may also be to visualize that which you seek. By continually seeing yourself as a doctor or a lawyer, you begin to accept it as a reality. This overcomes any old limiting beliefs that you are incapable of becoming such an esteemed person. The old adage "fake it until you make it" is really talking about using intention through visualization to manifest.

Free will or predestination?

What a lot of people call "free will" we refer to as the freedom of choice to decide the course of action you will take in any situation. The whole premise around entering into any duality is that you may have choices. These choices facilitate the lessons you came to learn. If you had no free will or freedom of choice, you would be nothing more than an observer. If you have no selection concerning your actions, why not just stay at Home and watch others tackle the same lessons and see how things turn out for them?

But what happens if you are on the couch or the sidelines just watching what is going on in the game? You never feel what it is like to accomplish something. You see others making touchdowns and winning awards but you don't know what it is like. In order to really feel and learn the lesson involved you must arrange a situation in which you can receive the sensations yourself.

What the soul plans while still at Home is the type of lesson it wishes to learn. It may seek to experience being controlled by another, being abandoned, feeling isolated, being dependent. What is not decided in advance is exactly how that lesson is going to be played out. The soul will be presented with numerous situations, each of which represents the energy sought to be understood, and the soul then chooses the scenario in which it wishes to engage. The experience of being controlled may come from living as a slave, an employee, an abused spouse, or a member of a military organization. Abandonment may come from being orphaned, having a spouse leave the relationship, having an employer go bankrupt, or something similar. These decisions are not made until you are incarnate, and they depend on what choices you make along the way concerning family members, spouses, employment, and the like.

Cut off from spirit

You are a soul. You are a piece of Source that broke off to gain knowledge for all. One of the universal projects that all souls undertake is to find out who they truly are. They plan a number of things to experience in each lifetime on Earth. They don't remember that when they start their life, because they come to their body with amnesia of anything they have done before this life. A soul is never alone or disconnected from the whole universal energy composed of all the pieces of Source.

When you "make contact" you acknowledge that feeling of your true self. Once you have learned something it is impossible to forget it. If you do not use your knowledge its intensity will seem to diminish, but it still remains. Remember, when you get used to something it is not always drawing your attention to itself. When people move near a railroad or under a flight path, they are constantly aware of the noise. But after they have been there for a while they don't hear it as being so annoying. Has the sound diminished? No, they just got used to its being there.

Spirit is always with you; it is a part of your essence. Two things will happen: you become used to the uniqueness of the connection, and you don't have a real need to feel that connection right now. Still, you may activate that feeling any time you are ready.

Awakening the kundalini

Kundalini energy is life-source energy, directly connected to your essence and, therefore, to the oneness of Source. To tap into this energy is the lifelong dream of mystics and aspiring masters. The name comes from the Sanskrit, meaning coiled—sometimes translated as snake. This refers to the fact that it remains coiled within the physical body until it is awakened through intention or by stimulation of some sort. Yoga practices, meditation, psychotropic drugs, and other means may cause it to uncoil and rise unbidden.

Since it is so powerful, it can affect the senses in all kinds of ways, including out-of-body experiences and psychic expansion. With discipline, the kundalini energy may be brought under control and used to connect to Source energy, your soul essence, and the unconditional love of the universe, generally called "bliss."

Kundalini energy is only dangerous when people get freaked out by its appearance and fight the effects. There may be a psychic break from third-dimensional reality, causing difficulties with everyday life. If they relax and meditate on these new, enlarged feelings, they will learn to control when it is active and how far it transports them into the other dimensions. If you suspect or are aware that the kundalini is causing you discomfort, you may use your intention to push it back into a coiled, non-reactive state.

The ascension process

First it is important to discuss the terminology involved in the issue of ascension. Many different groups and authors have used the terms ascension, kundalini, and enlightenment in a variety of ways, some of them contradicting their associates. We shall tell you how we are using the terms in this message.

By ascension we mean the ability of the soul, while still incarnate (and not having gone through a death process), to rise above the heavy, third-dimensional energy of ego and negativity into a state where it is possible to communicate with all the other souls who are not incarnate and to access all the wisdom of the universe. When ascended, the soul has the choice to maintain its physical body or to shed it and be in its formless, energetic condition. This takes place when the soul has completed its life lessons for that cycle. It may remain in contact with the Earth to be of service to other souls.

The kundalini is an energy of self (the soul or essence) that remains coiled within the body until acknowledged, and then is unhindered by human conflicts in its rise to conscious awareness. This may occur by stimulating the connection between yourself and Source energy or the universe, causing a connection with the unconditional love and bliss of your true state of being. It can be accomplished by working on yourself, or happens spontaneously as you complete your life lessons.

The process humans go through to reach ascension or a full kundalini rising is referred to as "enlightenment." People may be said to be enlightened, to a degree, when they have a knowledge and understanding of the essence of themselves, even if they have not gone all the way to ascension or bliss on Earth.

All souls are capable of reaching these stages during an incarnation if they have not burdened themselves with too many or complex learning experiences.

If you check online, many sites will give you a "process," or "characteristics" of a person undergoing the ascension process. Simply put, if you are learning your life lessons, getting to know your true energetic self, and continuing to disconnect as much as possible from third-dimensional ego, you are proceeding toward ascension.

Is this process a requirement in order to fulfill your life's mission? No. What will the result be for you if you manage to ascend while still in body form? You will have completed everything you came down to Earth to learn, and you may decide to return Home, remain here as a guide for others to accomplish what you have just done, go back and forth, or do whatever you wish.

Work to understand all your life lessons, connect with your Guides and other non-physical beings, rid yourself of ego, and recognize your true essential self; then you will be ready to ascend.

Chapter Five
Healing

Healing is the use of the love energy of the universe to balance the physical body. We have to understand the response of our mind that can create physical dis-ease—a lack of wellness. We must also understand the role played by energetic healers and by ourselves as conduits for the universal healing energy.

Energy and intention
Chakras
Chakra health
Sleep
Sound healing
Identifying with disease
Fighting depression
Controlled by fear
Is sickness inevitable?
Radio waves and blockages
Organ transplants
Trauma and body fat
Weight gain and self-love
Anger at current issues
Creating happiness

Energy and intention

Energy is everywhere. Everything that you can comprehend and everything that you can imagine is energy. The way you, as a human being, see something is based on the energy signature it chooses to possess. The workings of the human body are energetic and sometimes need assistance to get back into balance or to stay in balance. The free energy, that which is not contained in a physical format, is called universal life-force energy and functions to provide balance.

Illness, disorders, and physical infirmities are all the result of some thing or force blocking the free flow of energy throughout the physical body, creating dis-ease within the body. Healers call on the universal life-force energy, which is everywhere in creation, to release these blockages and restore the energy flow. The energy itself is "intelligent"—in other words, it cannot be used to harm another. Energy healing has been in existence for as long as there have been human bodies needing adjustment.

There are many recognized forms of energy healing and many practitioners of healing arts. Energy may be directed by intention. Different labels have been assigned to the process of directing energy by people who have found a procedure that works for them. They will then teach others how to do their procedure, calling it Reiki, Deeksha, Qigong, Therapeutic Touch, or any one of a number of titles. The commonality between them is the direction of universal life-force energy to free blockages within the body.

By itself, the universal life-force energy is intelligent. It knows where to go and what to do when directed to enter into a body, and will do just that unless the intention of the director pushes it to do something more than balancing the body. And, by itself, the energy will do no harm and is always "of the Light." It is not necessary for you to believe in each practice in order for it to help you. You merely need to be open to the process. As we always say to you humans, "Get out there and go with the flow!"

The process is a very simple one: The practitioners, who have a proper intention to help others, pull energy through their own bodies in order to harness it before directing it to their clients. There is a little more to it than that. Practitioners must have their clients' highest and greatest good in mind, and the client recipients must also want to overcome their affliction. In some cases individual clients may not be ready to finish with the ailment they are facing; they may have more to learn from the experience.

Since the energy is directed by the intention of the healers, their intention holds the key to the workings of the energy. Most healers hold the intention that everything they do is for the highest and greatest good of their clients. If the practitioners have an agenda of making clients dependent upon them, they will put restrictions or negativity within the energy flow. They will also believe that *they* are doing the healing, when in fact, any healing done is the work of the universal life-force energy and they are merely a conduit for that force.

When becoming involved with energy healing, it is always imperative that you determine the intention of the healers. Talk with them and see if they are controlled by their ego or by the pure intention of helping others. See if they are talking about bringing you into balance or if are they setting up a prolonged business for themselves requiring many treatments before they even begin. If so, it is the energy that is not of the Light but of the practitioners.

Many have ritualistic practices intended to prepare students to be healers. When students think this is necessary, they will not believe they can direct energy until they have gone through that special process. Once they have been inducted into the practice, they finally activate their intention and the energy flows. Even if you have never taken a single energy class, if you have the intention to heal with energy, you have the ability to do so. The next step is what the client's intention is for the energy—but we will discuss that elsewhere.

Chakras

Chakras are the energy centers regulating the flow of energy within the physical body. There are seven major centers, which have been studied at length for their effect on the body. The heart center of these bodily vortexes is the central point in the energy cycle. The physically dominant centers are below the heart and the spiritually dominant are above the heart. The heart has aspects of both; it is the organ that keeps the body functioning and is the repository of the feelings of the soul.

When you leave the physical body and venture into the non-physical realms of the person, you enter into an entirely different and additional set of chakras. The higher heart chakra is part of this etheric rather than the physical system. If you laid the etheric pattern over the human body, the higher heart center would be in the thymus region.

Although it is positioned outside the physical body, the higher heart center, like the heart center, is all about regulating experiences felt by the body. These have more to do with the mental and emotional aspects of living and learning than the physical ones.

In addition to the patterns of the main chakras, there are layers that radiate out from the body, creating a series of shell-like coverings. Each layer is subtly related to the spiritual path that the soul has entered. The circles closer to the body relate to the most physical and those farther out to the most spiritual.

All physical chakras relate to life lessons the soul has undertaken. The spiritual chakras relate to the connections the soul has between its current physical life and all its previously learned experience, as well as the awareness of its essence that it has been able to bring into the physical life. The more spiritually aware people become, the more they are connected to the universal oneness.

Chakra health

Chakras are energy centers. Some of them are within the physical body and some within the non-physical body. Those affecting human health are the physical chakras. There are seven physical chakras, extending from the root chakra at the base of the spine up to the crown chakra exiting out the top of the head. The chakras are connected by what is called the pranic tube. This tube carries force energy up and down the length of the body.

A blockage in any chakra affects the rest of the body because all is interconnected. It is important for health reasons to ensure that the chakras are all rotating with a flow of energy and that none is under- or over-active. Energy-sensitive persons will be able to tell you if your chakras are in proper tune. They may do this with their hands or a pendulum. They will also be able to help you balance your chakras using their hands, intention, a pendulum, or vibrational sound.

This is a very brief and simplistic look at chakras, but know that if they become blocked they can stop the flow of energy and cause dis-ease within the body. The very least that you should do is, during meditation, visualize the energy flowing freely up and down your pranic tube, rotating the chakras like little engines supplying energy to your entire body. This will help promote health and balance within your body.

Sleep

Each human body has a different mechanism requirement. Some bodies are well-tuned machines running like race cars, others are average energy producers and have satisfactory output, while still others have clogged electrical and fluid systems and just barely chug along. Human beings have to generate sufficient energy to balance their internal systems.

An average human body needs to have regular maintenance, and part of that is the daily recuperation period of about six to eight Earth hours. During this sleep cycle, in addition to recharging the physical body, the soul may huddle with its advisors and go over the game plan for the next time period in the body's life. Since the consciousness of the person has to maintain its amnesia to get the most out of lesson learning, any consultation with the Home team must be done while the conscious mind is asleep.

If the soul has completed the majority of its lessons, or has entered into a phase of helping others and is not continually working upon itself, it can go into a quick-charge mode, which just replenishes the body. Einstein was one of those taking quick, 15-minute naps to rejuvenate his cellular materials, after which he would jump right back into his work.

Just as a body that has gone through a trauma needs a large amount of down time, so also do some souls' bodies that are working through carry-over lessons from past lives. These particular people may even require nine or ten hours of sleep a night. This is similar to the needs of developing children who must put additional energy into the structural components of their growing body to have the strength to continue on their life's journey.

It is always possible to use your mental abilities to change the needs of the body, but be careful of what the body is involved in at the time. You may be diverting it from a necessary function. Freedom of choice allows you to set your own rules for any phase of your growth.

Sound healing

We would like to mention the "healing circle" concept and the power that it creates. Whenever you have a group with a central intention, such as the healing of a particular client or the balancing out of a situation, the energy the group generates is much stronger than the sum of the individual parts. This combined effort has the ability to move mountains, as any recipient of a group healing, who participated with total openness and acceptance, can affirm.

To understand the effect that musical vibrations have upon the human body you need only remember that the human body is mostly water. Take a bowl of water and blow softly across the surface, and the water will ripple and pulsate to the flow of your breath. If you float on a wavy body of water such as a pool, lake, or ocean, every molecule of your body is aware of the movement.

Music creates sound waves that are felt by the body and have the effect of balancing or disrupting the tissue. Kidney stones may be broken up while inside the kidney by the application of sound waves that cause the stones, made out of minerals, to disintegrate.

The chakras, the major energy centers within the body, each vibrate to a different tone. Using a singing bowl, tuning fork, or musical note produced by an instrument can cause the chakra to vibrate in synchronization with that frequency, which balances the flow of energy throughout that section of the body. Each chakra is closely associated with glands, and balancing the chakra has an impact upon the associated glandular system.

Mantras and chanting can produce a multitude of vibrations that clear, balance, connect, and carry intentions.

Drumming causes a vibration that can approximate the rhythm of Mother Earth. It is very calming, and it is possible to float on the sound and have a fantastic meditative trip. You are hearing more about all of this now because people no longer fear what they don't completely understand and are willing to accept anything that might be of assistance to them.

Identifying with disease

A diagnosis is an evaluation of the progression of various conditions within a human body. It is based on the observations of other patients who have received the same diagnosis. It is by no means a sentence, nor is it an absolute statement that <u>all</u> pathways are identical.

Do you accept that you have a specific condition? Do you expect your progression to be identical to whatever is reported in the textbooks? Then you can do nothing but sit back and wait for it to happen. You have identified yourself as having a condition, claiming that you are the same as all the others with that condition.

Haven't you heard of people who were given three months to live, yet here they are ten years later laughing at the stress they made themselves endure until they chose to take control of their own destiny? Be it diabetes, arteriosclerosis, heart conditions, or any other medical malady, unless you identify yourself with it, claim it, or call yourself its disciple, you are not fully under its domination.

Live each day as it comes. Have a positive attitude toward your life. See and project yourself outwardly with the love and beauty you possess within, and you will be living your own life as you planned it, not as a projection from a textbook.

Fighting depression

Human depression is an interesting state. Take the word apart: you have the prefix "de-," the word "press," and the suffix "-ion." "De-" means "the undoing, reversing or ridding of something"; "press" means "to urge onward"; "-ion" means "the process of." So the word depression means: "the process of losing the urge to move forward." The driving force in your life has been turned off.

For the soul this state is potentially as good as society sees it as bad. The soul views the depressed state as the ultimate moment of choice. All the governors in your life have been removed. There are no more commands coming from outside telling you what to do. There is a vacant space where those orders usually reside. This allows you to start all over again, making only decisions you have freely chosen, placing them in the vacant space, and reinventing your definition of self.

You may experience depression not only from losing your job, but any time you complete a lesson and no longer have it urging you onward. Students may find themselves depressed after graduating. Depression is commonly felt after divorce, particularly by a woman who has been a stay-at-home mother. The loss of family members whose care has been labor intensive can bring depression, not relief. In each case it is time to start over again.

For those who have no concept of their self-worth starting over brings a feeling of devastation. For those secure in their own power, however, it is freedom. Depression should be looked upon as an opportunity. You have swept the house clean, so now decorate it as you see fit. Start with an inventory of your abilities, your tools, and your desires. Plan where you want to go and begin the trek.

The first step to success is living in the moment. Don't spend time blaming people or condemning yourself—what is done is done. Seize the opportunity to showcase your strengths. Don't be afraid to follow your feelings into new arenas. You have nothing to lose and everything to gain by being your new self.

Believe that you can feel good; then you can see what it is like to feel good, and ultimately move into feeling good at will. Once you believe, you can change your thinking to *knowing* that you can feel good any time you desire. When you know you can feel good, whenever that sense of depression or self-loathing arises, go from thinking to acting. Already knowing it is possible to feel good, concentrate on that feeling and then start feeling good. You will reach a point where you feel good all the time because you do not want to feel any other way.

(Publishers' Note: *This discussion does not aim to give medical advice. If you are feeling depressed we suggest you consult with a licensed medical practitioner.*)

Controlled by fear

Some of you experience an intense need to know what is coming next. You feel that you are not in control of your life, imagining all the worst possible scenarios that could befall you. And because your mind is so powerful, you actually empower the things that you fear the most. So your fear turns the feared event into a reality.

This fear originates from expectations that you have for the outcome of everyday activities when you don't feel in control. Start by realizing that control is an illusion. It is simply impossible to make free decisions for all the people who are involved in your day-to-day life. In fact, you can only make your own action choices. Stop trying to micromanage and direct the universe. Have faith in your soul's existing choices for your Earth lessons. You did not plan more for yourself to experience than you are capable of handling.

When you fixate upon an event (accident, illness, or frightening thing), you so anticipate it that you place yourself into an environment for it to occur. Stop looking for these things and they will not appear in your life. Of course, death will definitely happen at the appropriate time—a time you have pre-selected. But what is there to fear about going Home? Back to a place where you are loved unconditionally? Where you are reunited with all your soul mates and your twin flame? When the time is right you will *welcome* death.

Is sickness inevitable?

Some people are said to have a "genetic predisposition" to an affliction, such as breast cancer, that has run throughout a family because they share the same common human gene pool. That said, we assure you that you have the freedom of choice to select your experiences during each lifetime.

You may have selected this particular family either so that you could experience this ailment, or so that you would be in a situation of having to deal with the emotion of having many close relatives being afflicted in this way. You must understand, however, that you do have the ability, both on a conscious and on an unconscious level, to prevent certain disorders from entering your system if you do not need to have that particular experience.

You may also rid yourself of disorders that have impacted your body if you understand why you chose them in the first place; you then no longer need to deal with them. The reason you elected to have an experience may be that it can help you to define feelings about yourself, or it may prove to you that you really can reverse adverse situations.

Your entire human life is but one lesson that keeps changing and evolving. You are the designer, architect, builder, maintenance personnel, and the owner of your life's journey. Enjoy your happy, fulfilling trip.

Radio waves and blockages

Human beings have varying sensitivities to energy. Some people can lie under high tension wires and feel absolutely nothing and experience no side effects. Other people develop blockages within their bodies, frequently diagnosed as cancer, when they are merely in the vicinity of those same energy fields. This has also been known to occur in susceptible individuals from exposure to television sets and computer terminals.

A cell phone is both a receiver and a transmitter that captures and generates energy fields. As mentioned above, people may spend their entire waking life with the phone glued to their head and suffer no ill effects, or use the phone once and create an energy blockage. Since the entire human body functions with electrical impulses, anything that changes or impedes the flow can be felt—subject to people's awareness of their physical and non-physical body.

Some people become hypersensitive to wave-form energy. They may develop a very keen sense of the flow of the pranic (Chi) energy throughout their chakras and body. What they might then perceive would not be recognized by the majority of the population. As we have mentioned before in our post on the chakras, keeping them clear and moving can be done by meditation, visualization, intervention of an energy worker, or intention. Building up a full, steady flow of energy through the tube will help clear the crown chakra.

Organ transplants

Every soul brings to itself that which it wishes to experience. If it has chosen to deal with the breakdown of the physical body and all the implications of such a condition, for example being in need of an organ transplant, that is how its incarnated life will look. If a family loses a loved one in some type of an accident that leaves most of the vital organs intact, one of the issues they have chosen to deal with is whether to allow parts of their loved one to go on living in the body of another.

Nothing is right or wrong. Having the ability to artificially prolong the time spent in one lifetime is all part of the initial plan envisioned before coming to Earth. Every aspect of a transplant scenario, on both sides of the transference, has a lesson involved.

A transplant does not involve just the donor and the recipient. It encompasses the transplant team, the families of both, and everyone who knows or comes into contact with the parties. For each individual, it creates different learning experiences around issues such as grief, relief, worthiness, their religious beliefs, and accepted ethical implications for their own spiritually planned life. These are personal lessons for each. They should be embraced, studied for the energies involved, and used to learn more about the self as a divine soul.

Trauma and body fat

Belly fat or any fat within the physical shell is in the physical body, and the etheric body is part of the non-physical self. While it is true that past-life events and lessons that were not cleared and are held in the etheric body may have an impact on the physical body, there is not an absolute correlation between body fat and underlying hidden issues. A body condition does not impact a non-physical problem.

One way to hold on to the fat is to believe that there is a correlation between unsolved problems and girth. If you made a contract before coming to Earth to have weight as a guidepost for you to determine your progress through your lessons, then it would work in that way. You could also convince yourself there is a connection between unresolved issues and holding the energy of them in the form of fat.

Other factors come into play. Eating is a comfort activity for humans, and fat is seen as a protection from many negativities. Past lives involving starvation or gluttony may be impacting your impression of yourself unconsciously.

Weight gain and self-love

Many energetic patterns are currently making the rounds among souls on the planet. Those who are openly sensitive, such as Indigos, Crystals, Stars, and Lightworkers, are feeling a sense of being ripped apart or picked up by the flow and being blown all over the place.

One of the unconscious automatic responses is to weigh yourself down so you are not so drastically affected. Hence, a lot of souls, who are not merely affected by the horrid diets that Earthlings have adopted, are putting on weight to keep themselves in physical reality—or grounded, as you might say.

This is, however, an unconscious act. It makes it easier for souls to go through their lessons because they aren't thinking about themselves, just what is happening to and around them. When they open up their view to include the physical container they are wearing, their human body, they are aghast at what they have allowed to occur. Their response, then, is to hate the physical and retreat more into the spiritual, which is non-judgmental. What is happening is a rejection of the love of self that is an aspect of true enlightenment.

Explore that aspect of yourself which is self-love. Accepting the love within will enable you to take the steps necessary to change your current appearance. Realize that you are a piece of Source and are all-powerful and magnificent. As such, you may create any reality that you wish. In the physical, this reality must include the discipline necessary to see a result. Intention is only the spiritual side; exercise and a healthy lifestyle are the physical side. Love yourself enough to change. Feeling miserable only makes you seek more physical comfort, which equals favorite foods. Allow only positive thoughts into your day.

Anger at current issues

The awareness that many have of the planetary issues is the result of media coverage, which has increased exponentially. In recent years politicians, in particular, have jumped on the bandwagon that makes the most of disasters and deplorable conditions—all with the statement that they alone can offer a solution for the problems. Cynics say we have only ourselves to blame and no one is able to correct the problems.

With people pointing out all the failures in the world that could possibly exist, and thousands giving support to one plan or another, coupled with the observation that nothing is really changing for the positive, the result is predictable: Anger, frustration, and sadness are to be expected if you are invested in the society in which you live.

When you are consumed with all these physical actions, it is impossible to see the spiritual aspects of the causes. Making this your accepted environment and choosing to feel affected by it, without recourse, will make your life even more chaotically third-dimensional. Souls create what they want as their environment.

We always tell souls: You are exactly where you need to be when you are there. How you feel is how you choose to feel. That is the spiritual lesson here. Learn to create rather than being manipulated by the words of others. Feel the unconditional love of your soul and adopt that as your day-to-day sensation. What is happening in the world is the result of the choices of the other people with which you share the planet. Let them feel the devastation if they need. Go to your higher spiritual self and bask in love, knowing that what is happening is needed by others but not by you.

Creating Happiness

There are three easy steps to being in a good mood and feeling great all the time. First, you must create an environment where you think happy thoughts. When you are remembering the best times you have ever experienced, you can't be unhappy, so any time you feel yourself getting depressed, take the time to relive the best possible experience you remember having had. Bring that happiness forward into the present.

Second, act as if you are happy even when you don't feel like going into the past and the present is bugging you. Every time you meet people in a store, on the street, or in an elevator, greet them pleasantly and wish them a glorious day. You will find it impossible to remain a sourpuss yourself when you're busy cheering up others.

Third, walk away from negativity. When your coworkers are in the lunchroom gossiping about or criticizing another employee, walk away. Do not stay in that negative area—and please, never participate.

When you live life by these three steps you will find your bubbly, happy self, which has always been just under the surface. You will notice that you have much more energy—it burns up much more of your energy to be gloomy and hateful than to smile and laugh.

Chapter Six
Life Lessons

Questions about our life lessons abound in the Masters' contact with incarnate souls. It is very puzzling to human beings to be told that they have actually chosen to experience suffering or to cause suffering in others. The Masters hammer home their answer in a variety of ways to make sure we all get the message.

Life purpose
The reason for life lessons
Identifying life lessons
Completing life lessons
Conflicts and the soul
Whatever comes your way
Chosen or determined?
Suppressed emotions
Completing contracts
The soul's pathway
Obsessed with money
Addiction to pornography
Information from the past
How you love yourself
Sitting back and doing nothing

Life purpose

"What is my life purpose?" is a frequently asked question. Most people seem to think that if they are unaware of their purpose in life, they are doing something wrong. Let us repeat one of our mantras: "Nothing is right or wrong." And another: "You are always exactly where you need to be to learn the lessons you sought."

When you decided to make a trip to planet Earth, which we call incarnation, you didn't do it on the spur of the moment with no thought or planning beforehand. You researched all the possible things you wanted to experience within the duality of Earth, and what you would most like to learn. These situations are called life lessons. You queried your advisors—your council of twelve souls who had studied the same types of lessons before you—and your various soul mates. Only then did you decide what you wanted to do. The lessons you chose are the purposes you have in incarnating and then reincarnating again.

To ensure that you would experience those desired lessons, you made contracts with other souls to help you set up the necessary staging for the events. Some of the incidents would be considered as positive in the human realm and others as negative. Your purpose was to figure out what you wished to learn and then, in understanding it, find the wisdom beneath that could be applied to all other events in your soul's continuing lifetimes.

The one purpose you *always* incarnate with is to find what it is that you wanted to accomplish. If we told you the specifics of each lesson you had decided to learn, you would be missing half the process. When you were in school, if the teacher had only given you the answers to questions without first asking the questions, you would have learned nothing. For us to tell you the purpose you had in mind would be the same. So we say, "Discovering your purpose is your purpose."

The reason for life lessons

We wish to discuss with you something we hear from your planet so often: the phrase "Why did I choose to come and experience this horrible life lesson?" This is frequently accompanied by despair and a sense of hopelessness.

Let's review the basics of human existence. When the soul is at Home in its purest form, it resides in total unconditional love just like the Source from which it broke off. In order to appreciate the magnificence of self, the soul may choose to come down to planet Earth into a duality where every emotion and experience has an exact opposite. Exposure to that which is the opposite of unconditional love can awaken an appreciation of what has been lost.

To provide an example, let's just say that you live in a land where it is hot and sunny every day. You think this is marvelous but admit that it is a bit boring to have the same monotonous weather day after day. One day you move to the South Pole with its sub-zero temperatures, winds that threaten to remove your coat, and blowing ice that obscures the sun. Then you really know what you have lost! So had you not chosen to go and experience something different on Earth, you would never fully realize the perfection of Home.

Before entering into a human shell and coming to Earth to live out a lesson, you observe all the possible things that are less than perfect. Without trying each one, though, it is just like reading something in a book but never having firsthand experience of it.

For instance, marathons fascinate you; you can read all about them and watch them, yet never take part. Do you know what it is like to run a marathon? No! Until you have done the training, run the miles, felt the exertion and exhaustion, it is merely a concept. Train for and run a marathon, and you gain the wisdom of the experience.

Human life is the only way for your soul to gain the wisdom of the knowledge that has come to you. Experience the occurrence so that you may evaluate it to know whether you want to experience it again. That is a life lesson.

Identifying life lessons

You already have signposts in your life that say "this is a life lesson." Never seen them? Of course you have, but you have just not recognized them. Any time you have a fear in life, or a doubt about what action you should take, you are face to face with a lesson. Just take your time and work through each task.

When you become aware of fears and doubts, stop for a moment and ask: Where does this come from? How do I feel about this fear? Does it relate to some other experience I have had and avoided? Do I think of something that seems totally unrelated, like a statement about my abilities from the past? Delve deeply into the feelings surrounding each fear and doubt—those are the outlines of your learning session.

All the fears and doubts belong to you; you have plenty of things to do for yourself—no chance to get confused with someone else's lessons. Nothing is too harsh for you, because you never set out to be confronted with more than you are able to handle in a lifetime. Take and clear each concern as it arises. It is not necessary to identify the lessons by definition, such as: this one is about abuse, that one about ego.

When you reach a state of being at peace with your life, no longer facing doubts and fears, you have completed this life's desired work. Then playtime may commence!

Completing life lessons

Is it possible to complete all possible life lessons a soul may choose to experience in Earthly incarnations in one lifetime? Not without living the equivalent of hundreds of lifetimes in one body. The other way to look at the issue is: Is it possible for a soul to complete all the life lessons chosen for its lifetime, the average single span of a body, within that one lifetime? The answer is a resounding Yes!

Some of the Masters spent periods of time on Earth far exceeding the normal human life span, which enabled them to work on many different lessons. But even they reincarnated at other times because they could not fit all the possible scenarios into one lifetime. To gain all the knowledge of negativity on Earth, you must experience each of the body's sexes. Limiting events generally require physical or mental inadequacies, while manipulation requires above-average intelligence. Physical experiences require a whole body.

Enlightenment comes when the conscious mind becomes aware of the unconscious, non-physical aspects of the soul. To speed up the process within a life, rid yourself of doubts and fears; turn from the ego judgment of the physical dimension to the unconditional love of the spiritual dimension. Tune into the universe and enter the energetic flow. Give up control, the need to know, and expectations. Have faith and trust in your feelings, not your mind. In other words, get to know the true essence of your loving soul while still incarnate.

Conflicts and the Soul

On a soul level we do not judge things to be "good" or "bad." That does not mean that your soul while incarnate on the planet cannot sense the energy of society in judging things that way. But it also means that a soul has the choice *not* to get involved in things outside its lesson plan. Such a non-interactive choice is not to be confused with refusing to be concerned or absolving oneself from any blame for not jumping into the fray.

The soul cannot have the full human experience unless it has an aspect of self that is ego based. If the soul remained

95

completely bathed in unconditional love it could experience nothing. Some of the lessons that a soul chooses to learn deal with an interaction in the physical and emotional traumas impacting people around them. However, many soul lessons involve only the soul's personal interactions with others.

When the soul lesson involves a larger group of players, this may lead to an investment of time and money to support one side or another in a conflict, actively protesting the actions of one group, or even diving physically into the conflict on behalf of one party. These must be the tests along the soul's path or they become a diversion and will slow down the soul's journey to wisdom. Some souls become so involved in this fashion that they do not face the challenges they came to Earth to complete.

Remember, each soul makes its own choices. One soul cannot make choices for another. To get entwined in a conflict, speak out about it, or protest the actions of a group, may be part of a lesson in self-worth, or a recognition of your own power, or a refusal to be controlled by another, or even the experience of getting sucked up in a group hysteria.

Whatever the true reason for a soul's activity, the worth may be evaluated by going inside and asking, "Why am I doing this? What do I seek to gain myself out of this action?" If the answer has to do with a lesson or emotion you are trying to understand, it is part of your journey. If the answer is to "show" those people, examine your motives because you are mirroring something you need to face about yourself

Whatever comes your Way

We frequently hear the question "How are we supposed to know what life lessons we are here to learn?" We hear it from young and old, all nationalities, all practicing religious beliefs, and just about everyone in human form. Well, fasten your seat belts because we have the answer:

Whatever comes your way is what you need to experience.

What you need to experience is what you planned to learn before you came down to Earth. You selected all the categories of lessons you wanted to have, once you were in body form, and so you set up the sequences of events that would precipitate them. When you arrived on Earth you had amnesia so that you could face the lesson without previous knowledge and, in working through the lesson and understanding it, grow in wisdom, which was your ultimate goal.

The reason this question appears so frequently is that humans need reassurance that they are right. The soul doesn't judge things as right or wrong. The soul wishes to experience things so that it may gain wisdom through evaluating whether the action is something it wishes to repeat, or whether it has learned enough to move on.

Your human need for constant validation gives your power to "those who know" so that you can be sure you are "right." What hogwash! Honor yourself! Take responsibility for your life, and work through what is in front of you so that you can move forward. Go inside and follow those feelings that tell you the direction you intended to take.

Chosen or determined?

When you get ready to come down to Earth to learn some life lessons, you decide which ones you wish to encounter. These can be such things as anger, betrayal, romantic love, issues around self-worth, being controlled or controlling others. What you don't generally decide is exactly how you are going to experience these lessons.

Let us say that you are working on self-worth issues, and your basic premise is that you cannot accomplish anything because you are poor and stupid. You can continue to replay those identities for the entire lifetime, or you can start to find ways to change your impression of yourself.

The predestination crowd would say you planned to be dumb and poor. However, exercising your free choice, you might read a book on affirmations and begin to tell yourself you are brilliant, and that your brilliance may enable you to become rich. You start to excel at school, get a fellowship to do research, get national recognition, and win monetary prize after prize. You have manifested a realization about your self-worth by using your abilities to be recognized as brilliant and, in consequence, become wealthy.

If you follow only your thoughts, you make it impossible to change your feelings about yourself. These thoughts are a combination of dreams, expectations, and what you have absorbed from seeing, hearing, and reading what *other* people think. You may imagine that these thoughts (although not really yours) are pre-ordained and nothing you say or do will change them.

You acknowledge that your confusion arises from whether to exercise freedom of choice by seizing your own power, or sit back and accept what others plan for you, but you are the master of your soul. You alone are the driver of each lifetime. You alone determine the pathway, whether by manifesting what you would like to experience, or by sitting back and taking whatever comes.

Take responsibility for your actions today—don't worry about tomorrow. As each day dawns, live in the moment. When you try to figure out what you might have had in mind when you presented yourself with a series of lessons, you are worrying about the past and not living in the now. Choose what feels right in this moment. You are then manifesting what will help you increase your wisdom. That will be creating and walking your path.

Suppressed emotions

All souls have many layers of feelings and the sensation of many different dimensions within which they co-exist. When you are without judgment and ego, you are living outside the plurality of the Earth experience and are in touch with unconditional love where all is "heavenly."

As you get more comfortable in being free of duality lessons, which all souls come to Earth to experience, you open yourself to deeper levels of suppressed emotions and lessons from both your current and past lifetimes. As these deeper layers of human emotions emerge, you react to them as you did to the surface emotions which you worked through and learned from.

What you need to do with these recently dug-up feelings is to go into the thought process that accompanies them and see why you have returned to negative feelings. You are re- experiencing worthlessness and guilt, common Earth lessons.

You have worked through these many times before and will easily do so this time. You simply have to confront the feelings that come along with the emotions, take back your power to decide what effect they are going to have upon you, and reclaim your own identity.

These experiences can only be had in a world of judgment where some things are good and others are bad. Either see them as just challenges that you wish to have again (so you can keep them around), or learn why you never want to go through them again (so you can send them packing).

Completing contracts

We wish to talk about completing the contracts that you entered the Earth plane to fulfill. You may have looked upon these as life patterns or even as aberrations along life's pathway, but, in fact, these are your life lessons.

You made arrangements with some of your friends in soul form to help you experience various challenges. You may have wished to feel what betrayal, abandonment, upheaval, or a sense of loss is like. You didn't always determine the exact manner in which the lessons would be played out, but just the end result. Betrayal may be a broken promise to a child, a cheating husband, or false accusations from a close colleague. Abandonment may be your partner or parent's walking out on you, or the death of a close family member or friend.

Being in the midst of a devastating natural event, or being uprooted as a child by your parents to move to another location may be your expression of upheaval. You can experience a sense of loss from the death of a parent, child, or pet, or the cessation of your employment. Each of these examples affords you the desired lesson.

What do you do once the event is completed? That's the other side of the equation. These experiences are called life lessons because you came to Earth to learn from them. In each of these scenarios if you fight the emotions and feelings that come during the experience, you do not allow yourself to learn.

You must embrace the energy of the experience so that you have an imprint of its power—then you will not need any further examples of that lesson. If you do not embrace the sensation, you do not make a record of the feeling, and so you must go through the experience again until you allow yourself to feel.

The soul's pathway

We begin by speaking of lessons. This brief definition will help to bring you into synchronization with us. The way souls gain wisdom is by experiencing things. The sole purpose for souls' breaking off from Source is for them to gain experience outside of Home, which is the dimension of unconditional love. This we do with lessons, for souls to experience the positive/negative duality of the physical plane in which you live.

Lessons are not undertaken in a chance "whatever may come" fashion. They are pre-selected by each soul before it embarks on its journey to Earth. We all have advisors, guides, and a council who help us decide what to experience, but each individual soul makes the final selection of the lessons it wishes to learn.

We will review the duration of a lesson from planning to completion, taking the example of control, at its extreme, by one soul over another. In the comfortable energy of Home, we discuss what would be interesting for us to experience.

To know what it is like to be controlled by another, we have many different choices, slavery being one. For most of you, slavery brings to mind what happened in the Americas in your past, where a group of individuals went to impoverished nations, kidnapped people there, and forced them into servitude.

Slavery is only one form of personal control exercised over another, the taking away of what an individual soul believes to be its freedom of choice. Adult control may be exercised when a parent refuses to let her child choose a favored course of study at school, or engage in an after-school activity.

It may even begin with the consent of the one wishing to have the experience of being controlled, a perfect example from your past being indentured service. In this, souls gave themselves up to be the bonded servant of another for a set period of time so they might trade having no hope for their future for the chance of re-building their lives and bettering themselves.

A control situation frequently happens within your families when a child expresses an interest in a particular sport—tennis, soccer, or football. The parents think ambitiously and when their offspring shows talent, they become like masters dictating that, because the child is so proficient, he must continue to practice, even though he may not wish to continue the experience. So there are early-morning practices, and then more practices, and body-building, and a forced nutritional regime, all much beyond what the child ever sought to have. That sort of control is a kind of slavery.

How does this equate with the lessons we mentioned at the start? The soul has chosen to experience being controlled and giving up responsibility and freedom of choice to another. It may have given up control to avoid having to think or be responsible for what happens. Can this soul learn anything in that scenario?

The simple answer is that it can learn only if it realizes that it really does have a choice and can change the direction of its life by backing out of the agreement to be enslaved, or, in the sports example, by taking responsibility and telling the parents, "I do not choose to do that." The slave in chains may escape (as so many did). The indentured person may fulfill the contract and then move immediately to another location. People might learn why they have experienced a particular harshness if they go inside themselves to find the strength that is within. Having tapped into that strength, they will know it was a choice they made that, once experienced, does not have to be repeated.

If an incarnate soul is constantly fighting an experience, escape can be physical, mental, emotional, or by going Home—death. Many times when a soul, having experienced being controlled, is given the opportunity to move into a position where it is in charge of its own life, the fear of having to be responsible for itself keeps it in the same situation and it does not choose to move on.

The lesson for the soul is to recognize what it is doing in this lifetime, what it has experienced, and how it has the freedom of choice to learn not to be controlled by others. It can also recognize that it can make decisions and move from fear into acceptance of itself as an individual. Then it can finish the lesson by assuming responsibility for itself, heading off the control of another, and then advancing to the next chosen lesson.

Every soul in human form who is enslaved, whether in chains, or indentured, or under another's mental and emotional control, freely agreed before entering body form that it wanted to have that experience. It wanted to know what it felt like, wanted to know how it could change the tides and learn that it alone is responsible for itself, where it goes and what it learns.

So, although it may appear that those who are in chains have no choice, they actually chose to be born into that situation so they could experience that harshness. Within such lessons there are categories, control being the main one. Underlying that can be learning self-worth, for those who are enslaved frequently think that they deserve to be physically enslaved, until they learn that all of us, being part of Source, are the same.

Similar teaching experiences include souls' having to rely on other people. They may also involve aspects of illness in which, because of despair over their situation, people cut off the energy flow through their body and become critically ill. (They have the ability, if they go inside themselves, to learn that they can with their intention reverse the blockages they have created.)

Each of these experiences constitutes a lesson. Unless your soul taps your inner knowledge to find the basic experience you wish to have, and then completes it, you will not gain the wisdom of that experience. You may need to choose to revisit the same lesson in the same or a future life experience, until you have finally mastered it.

Obsessed with money

Some people are obsessed with money. These remarks are for them:

You judge your worth by the amount of money that you earn and possess. Will you be able to take any of this physical money with you when you return Home? No! Then why do you downplay the abundance of spiritual wealth you have that you *can* take with you?

Living in the third-dimensional human world, you judge your worth by the standards of society and what you see others possess. This is allowing society to create your belief systems for you. In this case it has to do with the amount of money you think you need.

Surround yourself with the unconditional love of your spiritual prosperity. The most balanced, spiritual, and happy people on your planet are those who possess nothing, like the Dalai Lama, Sai Baba, and cloistered monks. You do not have to emulate them—just stop falling on your knees before the altar of money.

Find your peace within the abilities that you have. Money problems are nothing more than an expectation of a want you believe you have. When you feel that you will not be able to devote yourself to spiritual matters until you have a big enough bank roll so you won't have to continue working, that money represents your worthiness. You are clearly stating to the universe and to yourself that you are not worthy to understand your life lessons. One of your lessons is understanding that obsession with money binds you to human need and prevents you from accessing spiritual wisdom.

Begin by having faith in your spiritual self. Your spiritual side knows the universe will provide whatever you need. It may not feel you have everything that you wish for, but you will have sufficient goods to spend time on your journey.

Addicted to pornography

Anything that causes a soul within a human body to lose control over the ability to stop a particular physical action is an addiction. Addictions are common life lessons in the book of soul lessons. Souls use human bodies to have senses with which to partake in physical actions and to feel the effect each has on the physical nervous system.

Many life lessons involve emotional stimulations such as fear, lack of self-worth, and lack of self-esteem. The totally physical sensations you have, which include anything to do with the pleasure senses, are the strongest things a human can feel.

When people are having problems accepting themselves and their progress in life, they engage in something that will take their mind off what else is or is not happening to them. Sexual release blanks out everything else, and for the moment makes everything seem perfectly wonderful.

That activity, done other than with another consenting adult, is seen by society as deviant. If you are still in the midst of ego judgment, you then condemn yourself for partaking. You are feeling so miserable because you don't understand the need for your addiction, and the addiction itself makes you hate yourself. Work first on accepting yourself. That is, love everything about yourself, since you are a soul gaining experience by undergoing lessons. When you can love yourself, you will not have the need to make yourself feel good physically because you will feel fantastic on an energetic level.

Information from the past

As the veil is thinning, more and more, Earthbound souls are reconnecting with those in non-physical form. Information from lives you have lived—things you have witnessed and experiences you have had—is coming back into consciousness. Things that are thrusting themselves at you at this time are assisting you to realize facts about yourself and your true essence.

While you are seeing these things for the events themselves, look at them instead for the feelings they engender within you. They are showing you your strengths, which you can use to get you through the transitions. They are also pointing out your weaknesses, lessons you have not completed, so that you may work on them.

Human life on the planet is cyclical. You lived during the last cycle, which is being repeated at this time, so you have an advantage in your memory cells. What you are experiencing is mainly for your benefit, but you may also assist others in their journey of enlightenment by telling them of your trials and tribulations and how they allow you to learn more about your soul. All of these things will become evident to you if you are open to the energy that accompanies each cycle.

How You love yourself

Spiritual love is easily acknowledged in your life when you totally accept yourself exactly as you are at the moment. Does it sound a bit strange to accept that you should love a body grossly overweight such that it is creating medical problems? What about accepting an addiction numbing you to your surroundings and separating you from the rest of the populace? Yes, we mean to accept all that is you! That is self-love. Self-love is unconditional love mirroring the Source energy of the universe. To not love the problem is to deny either that it exists or that you can learn enough to get rid of it from your life.

Self-love is relishing the reasons you have chosen to come into human form, in other words, acknowledging or being aware of your life lessons. It is only when you can step away from fighting what you are here to confront that you can begin the journey that gives you the knowledge and wisdom required by your soul.

Self-love means to accept—but not necessarily to "like"—the result or outward appearance of the lessons. This dislike becomes your motivation. You love that you have the strength to learn all about your lesson so you may reverse its deleterious effects upon your body. Love allows you to withdraw from the drama of the disliked task so you may dispassionately learn about it and find a solution to balance out the energy.

When you love yourself your lessons pop into awareness as difficulties in life—things you don't like, but for which, by jumping in and rummaging around, you may find the cause and, with that, a solution. It may seem elusive, but it is really right there in your face! As your "dislikes" lessen, your self-love thrives.

Should we just sit back and do nothing?

There are all different kinds of lessons that a soul may choose to experience on Earth. Yes, Earth is the only planet that has a dual energy setup, with both negative and positive conditions. Our lessons appear as negative energies and it is for souls to determine how to deal with those situations and make them into positive experiences to learn about themselves and their issues—if they can.

The above question would seem, for example, to imply that even a soul who chooses to be a doctor is interfering with the patient's life lessons. But life is much more complicated than that. The doctor cannot go out and drag in patients off the street and force them to receive medical treatment. All healing has to do not only with the actions of the healer, but with the intentions of the patient as well. If people do not want to be healed they will find a way to remain out of balance or at dis-ease with their body. Part of their lesson may be to acknowledge that they need the help of another. So, if people realize why they are suffering from a condition, they can go and seek out a healer who can assist in remedying the state.

In another example, good Samaritans might go to countries and help bring clean water to the people. After they leave, the inhabitants must maintain the water system; their lesson may be to take care of themselves.

Only in a situation where people are trying to force their beliefs and lifestyle on others can there be a case of interference. But don't forget freedom of choice—the recipients can always ignore the offered help. In a case where souls may be diverted away from their lesson by the assistance of others, they will have the ability to try again to learn the lesson in that same lifetime or another.

Chapter Seven
Planet Earth

We are inhabitants of a great, mysterious, and often frightening world. Paying lip service to our care for Mother Earth, we sometimes act like bullies and sometimes are full of fear concerning the changes in climate and the destructive power of earthquakes. The Masters answer many of our questions, including the 2012 issue, Lemuria and reptilians.

What is the world?
Living in the now
The environment
Helping Mother Earth
The weather
Climate change
Earth cycles
Disaster deaths
Haiti and 2012
Crop circles
Lemurians and Neanderthals
Are reptilians real?

What is the world?

We have used the word "World" in several different connotations in our communications. To begin this discussion, you must accept the concept that you are a soul having a physical experience, not a human that happens to have a soul.

Your soul needs to be part of a recurring illusion, a reproducible physical environment wherein it may begin a lesson in one lifetime, finish the physical duration of that particular body, and return to a similar environment to continue and hopefully complete that same lesson. The World was jointly created by millions of souls to be that physical place—a learning arena, but also a confinement.

We say "confinement" because it is a physical fixture and has a set position within the universe that is influenced by all the other masses in gravitational contact. Together these bodies set out the dimensions of time, the life of the human body, and a changeable living environment determined by your position upon the planet—all providing a stage for your play or reality. All you have to do is write the script.

The World comprises a duality with everything having an opposite. This allows freedom of choice—the learning from experiences that turns into knowledge, which on a soul level creates spiritual wisdom.

Living in the now

Time is a word that has many meanings on Earth. It basically describes a measurement used to understand a concept, such as how long it will take to grow an edible plant, or to travel from one spatial location to another. The premise is that these matters have a finite duration rather than an infinite one. You also have to be able to see the object in order to measure its movement and period of existence.

110

Humanity goes even further by recording past, present, and future occurrences using these measurements. When one talks about how long (in time) it took to get from one place to another in the past, how much shorter a period of time it takes now, and how it will be instantaneous in the future, one is using examples of time and, in the same instance, recording what one perceives as progress.

The soul and the energy around it that comprises the universe, are both infinite and therefore have no beginning, middle, or end points, so time does not exist for them. They are present in all that you on Earth see as time and in everything that has happened since your "time" began.

If a soul has experienced a human life and later wants to talk about the experience, it may do so in two different ways. Since time does not exist for the soul, it may concentrate its consciousness on the experience, and in so doing, jump back into the body and relive the exact moment in Earth time. Also, since the soul is not confined to a physical container (the body), it may split itself so it has all of its memories and knowledge intact, and reenter the body (where it has amnesia) with just a part of itself. The soul will still be able, with the remainder of itself, to monitor all aspects of the lesson the body has chosen to learn.

We experience time by being everywhere at once. We are in your past, present, and future. We are in all locations at once. We observe time by observing the changes that occur in each of you as you are affected by the passage of time on your planet. We are able to slide from one of your time periods to another to see what choices you make and how they play out. You may look upon it as possessing an embedded recording device that has everything that has been, is, or will be. We merely scroll through to watch your life.

Time is an invention of your world, used to help your memory differentiate the things you have done, and in what

111

order. Your measurement yardstick is the rotation of planet Earth around the Sun, so once you leave your planet it is no longer relevant. You use it to pressure yourself to complete this or that thing by such and such a date. The number of rotations since you came upon the planet—your age—determines what your society will or will not allow you to do: drink, drive, vote, or retire.

For the soul, however, the only important time is NOW! Allow your consciousness to focus on your immediate surroundings, drinking in all that is within view.

When you focus on time in any way you miss the Now. When you recall the past you miss the Now. When you strategize for the future you miss the Now. You will be missing this wonderful life you chose to experience. So take advantage of each moment and let your soul enjoy the Now.

The environment

Our question is whether you are living with your environment, squandering it, or are you fighting it? Your environment encompasses all the earthly physical elements that you come in contact with during your stay on the planet.

In the beginning, your species lived with the environment out of necessity. The use of electricity, natural gas, and other petroleum-based substances was unknown, and pollution was minimal. At first the building of shelter was unknown and naturally occurring land features, cliffs, caves, and large trees served the purpose. As man discovered ways to make or preserve fire, and started building structures out of rocks, trees, and animal hides he still lived in communion with his locale, but was able to better maintain his body temperature and health.

Initially man was a hunter gatherer and then found he could grow his own food with a little advance planning. He now had food, shelter, warmth, and a modicum of comfort.

Then he became greedy and began to gather and try to preserve as much as he could find, kill, or grow. In some cases he was successful and in others he wasted what he did not need. He didn't worry too much about despoiling the land because when it became foul he just moved on.

Next came mechanization and the ability to artificially produce just about anything. Want a constant temperature of 68 degrees Fahrenheit? Ignite the furnace or put more coal in the stocker. Ignore the fact that the by-product is pollution. Man began to get away from living with his environment and started using up the exhaustible resources of the Earth. He has become an unconscious unconcerned consumer. He takes what he wants and forgets satisfying needs. Man now squanders his resources and fights the cycles of nature.

Take a moment to think about this. Where are you in the scale of things? Do you care about the Earth or see it simply as your possession?

Helping Mother Earth

Earth has a finite amount of resources available to all the little creatures who inhabit her surface. Some humans feel the need to conserve and to reuse or recycle each finite resource; others couldn't care less whether they use all the potential of an item as long as the next needed item is available to them.

It would be lovely if souls came with in-built default settings to preserve planet Earth, but then what would they do with their freedom of choice? The trip to the planet is all about making decisions that allow us to learn from experience. Some lessons are what you consider good, and some are what most would term bad. But, alas, default settings would take away freedom of choice and so provide no human learning experience.

All you can do with your experience is to be true to your feelings. Live your life and create your reality using your personal freedom of choice to conserve, reuse, and recycle. Others may be moved by your example to pitch in and become more conscientious citizens.

Planet Earth is going through a lot of changes that you can readily see at this time. Part of what is happening is the regular cycle of renewal that takes place on Mother Earth. The planet is a live, breathing energy that is affected not only by her own cycles, but also by outside influences. The behavior of the little physical human beings running about on the surface of the planet has to do with their own egos and control issues.

As in the case of war and peace, it is impossible for one person alone to have any impact upon entire nations. It takes large groups of people with a concerted effort to affect the established energy patterns. You may send out an energy of gratitude for peace, because that will help counteract the energy of war. But if you pray, asking for peace, you are in effect telling the universe that you do not have peace, so you give more energy to its polar opposite— in other words you help create the energy of war.

Weather patterns result from planetary convergences, the placement of all the other planets in the solar system in relationship to Earth, and physical changes caused by humans. You cannot do anything to shift the positions of the planets in space unless you harness a massive amount of other people's energies together with yours. Without a concerted effort, the moon and the planets will continue to change the seasons and affect weather upon the planet.

Humankind has polluted a great deal of the air and the surface of the planet. If you were Mother Earth, would you stand quietly by and not acknowledge that you are being defiled? We don't think so. When construction creates strictures that are too binding, she responds with earthquakes, tsunamis, and floods. The result of your excessive physical demands is the pollution of the air, land, and water. You can still play your part by recycling and not using too much polluting fossil fuel.

Share your concerns with others. That being said, all souls have freedom of choice, so all you can do is inform those who will listen, practice what you preach, and send healing energy to Mother Earth. Remember, you chose to incarnate on the planet at this time to have the experiences you are living with today.

The weather

There is a lot of concern about your current weather. With all the talk about the greenhouse effect, pollution, and over-consumption, everyone seems to have a pet theory about the origin of this situation. A good number of people are campaigning to have governments and international corporations held responsible.

While we can confirm that all of the above-mentioned issues do have an effect upon the planet, they are not the only source of all the changes taking place. Planet Earth goes through cycles, each with certain characteristics, the best known being the ice ages, of which there is ample geological proof all over the planet.

Formation and reformation of the Earth's tectonic plates also have a major impact upon the weather. When the plates realign and a gigantic volcano spews huge amounts of soil and minerals into the air, the atmosphere is affected to such an extent that some species can no longer exist and new growth cycles have to evolve.

Planet Earth is also suffering cosmic stress from the positioning of the other celestial bodies in an array across the universe not seen in 26,000 years. These are all things that have affected Earth many times, but never before has the whole population been aware at one time of what is happening all over the globe. You have the news media to thank for this.

Just as you cannot single-handedly change the course of a raging river, you cannot "correct" what is happening on the planet. It is as it should be.

Climate change

The melting of the polar caps, often called global warming by you, is a cyclical event. It is influenced by many factors, the position of the sun relative to the Earth, the ozone layer around the poles, pollution which changes the temperatures of the oceans and therefore the activity of the jet streams, and planetary changes of the Earth herself, such as volcanoes and earthquakes.

If you compare the temperatures occurring on the planet at this time you will see that, while one area may have been several degrees colder, other areas have been warmer. Areas that normally have a lot of snow are barren, and other areas that usually get moderate snow have been buried. Air pollution has been an influence in this, as has the pull of other planetary bodies which are closer to the Earth than in recent years.

Global disaster will be wrought by something much larger than the minor temperature and weather fluctuations you are now seeing. If the inhabitants are not careful how they use the resources of the planet, they will become depleted and you will be unable to grow food or sustain animals.

It is important that people stop seeing things as endlessly available. Greed and selfishness are unbalancing the equilibrium of the planet. If each person sees not only his or her own needs but the needs of those around them and around the planet, and acts accordingly, everyone will have sufficient goods without depleting or polluting. It is only the attitude that "whatever it takes" to satisfy oneself is all right, without regard to the consequences, that has gotten your planet where it is today.

Work toward a carbon footprint that will sustain you without impacting nature. Do not waste, take only what is needed. Send spiritual energy to Mother Earth to help heal the crevasses and rifts that over-use have caused. Help to defuse the negative explosive energy causing eruptions of both earth and skin. Help everyone to form a womb of love and peace.

Earth cycles

The planet Earth is approaching a momentous time in its cycle within the solar system. One of the barriers that exist between our etheric dimension and your physical dimension is created by the magnetic and electric attractions among the other planets that bombard and affect Mother Earth. This has made it impossible for all but the most advanced souls to have ease in communicating between these dimensions.

Whole groups of humans are beginning to feel the Other Side through the thinning of the veil, as the planets across your galaxy start forming up in a straight line, which will be completed on the winter solstice in 2012. This is occurring because a harmony within all energy will be created when the formation is complete, and then all transmission interference will disappear.

In addition to feeling the vibrations, many people are sensing unrest within themselves and the need to move into different careers and pathways in their life. The predominant sensation being felt is one of anticipation. The urgency arises from the closeness in time to the event. This swing within the universe has been cycling for over 26,000 of your years.

Some of the feeling of desperation originates from the other side. Soul mates, old friends, and former companions are all waiting to re-establish contact. What you are waiting for is the ability to reach these souls who are calling out to you psychically. What you will be able to do, if you so choose, is to communicate with them and to bring forth your wisdom, which is stored in your Akashic records.

You are already sensing more of your essence, and this is pulling you away from the chaos that has recently been your life. With these attributes comes the confidence to follow what seems like a dream but is really your planned life path. Go with the flow! Open to, and trust in, this universal energy that surrounds you.

Disaster deaths

Recently we have been welcoming home large numbers of souls from their Earthly domain. The majority of these transitions has been the result of natural phenomena on your planet. Please know that all these souls had included their seemingly untimely death as a facet of their life lessons, and therefore had given prior consent to be a part of this mass exodus.

Some of these Earthly disasters have been caused by the planet's cyclical changes, and others are the result of its inhabitants' behavior. You are entering a period of time when many of these patterns of destruction will continue, but you are able to mitigate the intensity of some energy-related events with your intentions.

The way people are reacting in these trying times is allowing the energy to formulate patterns that will help them to change the governance of many nations. Earthly disasters are also causing all humans to examine their impact on the environment and to decide whether and how to change their behavior in relation to planet Earth.

Be conscious of the energy at this time, and you will move toward the discovery of your own creative powers.

Haiti and 2012

We have also been asked to comment on the happenings in Haiti. Many outrageous statements have been made by the publicity seekers of your world. These have ranged from "an agreement made with the devil" to a "man-made disaster" done for political reasons, plus some statements about aid being very publicly given in exchange for looking good in the world and future personal gain. We wish to clarify the occurrence since some aspects of these events, Haiti and 2012, are intertwined.

During the years we have been communicating with you, we have talked about many of the interconnected energies that have contributed to the current situation in Haiti, and changes on the physical plane leading up to the winter solstice of 2012.

Your planet's surface is composed of a series of geological plates that slide over, under, and around each other, referred to as tectonic plates. Several of these meet under the landmass upon which Haiti rides. One fault (the area where the edges of two plates come together) under the island has been building up pressure. Normally the plates slip a little against each other every year. This particular plate combination has been frozen for many years, creating an intense pressure.

The recent earthquake was a release of that pressure. Instead of moving fractions of inches a year, pent-up energy moved the plates almost six feet against each other, which resulted in a tremendous shifting along the entire plates and everything connected to them. The aftershocks were the motions of other landmasses along the plates that had not released with the first tearing. The Earth was shaking itself and stretching to release tight muscles, much like any other being that has become tense from having spent too long in a cramped position.

That is the physical cause and effect. Human energetic action also plays a part through the positive and negative energies generated by the incarnate souls existing in that area. We have explained in the past that planet Earth was set up as a place where a soul might go to experience all the facets of a particular lesson, such as love, hate, betrayal, control, and these can only be experienced in an arena of polar opposites. For each positive aspect on the planet there is an opposing negative aspect. One may not appreciate the positive aspect or the negative aspect unless one is able to see and experience its opposite.

These opposing energies are balanced—for all the good there is an equal amount of evil. When a person or group concentrates on negativity or evil, good energies are held at bay in that area. The practice of certain religious beliefs or rituals involves calling upon evil discarnates [*souls who have left their bodies but have chosen not to return Home to unconditional love*]. The religion aims to assist in obtaining power, control, and riches, and it gathers an extremely powerful negative energy.

This negative energy does in fact impact the flow of energy around geological areas of the planet. An easier way to understand this is to know that, like a person, the planet possesses an energy body. It is affected by the presence of negativity and responds to it. Although this is by no means the only cause, it has partially contributed to the stalling of the movement of the plates over the years, which has allowed the pressure to build up.

To reiterate, at this time in the history of your planet you are reaching a point in the 26,000-year cycle of the movement of planets in your solar system when they will reach a perfect alignment with the sun at the center, which will happen at the winter solstice on December 21, 2010, in your calendar. You are aware of the impact that your small moon has upon water on your planet by observing the daily tides. You also have observed the effect the full moon can have on the mental state of some people. Consider the multiplied potential effect of all the planets lining up across the galaxy, and you can understand the power that is beginning to be felt by you as a human being and planet Earth as an energetic body. Some of the planets in your system are reaching a closeness that occurs only every 26,000 of your Earth years.

This impacts everything.

In areas were negativity has stopped the balance of nature, the force of the universe to balance itself at this time of alignment will cause a lot of physical release to occur. This will be played out in such things as earthquakes, volcanic eruptions, floods, famine, starvation, and will affect the human psyche, resulting in terrorism and wars. On a spiritual level, people who are open to this new flow of energy will see that they are able to communicate through the energetic dimensions to seek advice from those souls and masters in non-physical form.

The powerful influence of this planetary energy has been building for several years and will be present for several years after the 2012 alignment. Incidents such as that in Haiti will occur again before this cycle is completed. Earth is stretching and balancing her energies. Souls may assist her by intentionally sending positive energy to her so she doesn't have to create such drastic events to reach stability.

On an individual level, be open to the flow of this empowered energy. Surround yourself with positive energy so the flashes of negativity will have no effect upon you. Join with others to send healing energy out into the masses to defuse some of the gathered hostility that exists. Use the now-available connections to the masters and guides to become ever more aware of your true essence as a soul.

Reach out to seekers around you and learn what they have been able to understand about the journey of the soul.

Find the purpose that brought you here. Inquire into the lessons you undertook during this life, which you may not completely understand. All of these things, and more, in the spiritual vein will be open to you if you seek them. Open your eyes, your mind, but especially your heart at this time to delve into your feelings, which connect you to all other souls on Earth and at Home.

Crop circles

Crop circles, other than those which are man made, are created by beings who are not of this physical cycle on the planet. Some are created by souls who have returned Home but still monitor the Earth and wish to help guide those who will listen by giving them scientific information. There are also souls in various guises who reside on other planets and want to be of service by leaving messages about happenings in the universe. All markings are left in friendship and good will.

Lemurians and Neanderthals

The Lemurians were a group of highly evolved creatures who had the ability to communicate with their minds and create whatever they chose to manifest. Unfortunately, part of the group decided they wished to play around with cold fusion, with explosive results. They broke up and sank their continent of Mu into the ocean. The westernmost edge is what is now known as the Hawaiian Islands, and the easternmost part is on the continental United States in the vicinity of Mt. Shasta, California.

Just before the catastrophe, a group of Lemurians migrated to the old volcanic tunnels within Mt. Shasta and other parts of California reaching toward the sea. They formed a series of cave dwellings which are called Telos.

They are in a slightly different vibration, so humans rarely see any of them.

Neanderthals, on the other hand, were a stage of progression in the evolution of today's homo sapiens. Sentience is the ability to be responsive to, or conscious of, sense impressions. We sometimes call it being "aware." Some people declare that a sentient being must be able to be empathetic to the plight of other beings.

The Neanderthals were progressing through this phase of growth. The shape of their brain had little impact on the development of this ability. The pre-frontal lobes held the group knowledge or instincts that the earlier man had worked through. The higher functions were being processed in other regions of the brain that previously had not been used. A combination of evolution and the periodic weather cycles caused the extinction of the Neanderthals.

Humankind is going through another evolution as we speak, opening what you call psychic pathways. To that end, you are redeveloping the skills of the Lemurian and Atlantean races. The size of your skull is deceptive because currently you are using such a small percentage of your brain. The changes occurring will activate a larger section of the brain and re-establish mind communication.

Are reptilians real?

Some urban myths about reptilian species have been propagating with increasing frequency. Ever since the introduction of the television series "V" some years ago, and its reemergence this year, reports of reptiles hidden in human coverings have flourished.

Is there a conspiracy of reptilian beings infiltrating the governments of the world? No.

Are they controlling the ruling bodies from an evil cabal? No.

Are there any species in the Universe that would appear reptilian to humans? Yes.

Do they have colonies on Earth? No.

Do they occasionally visit Earth out of curiosity? Yes.

Are there souls currently in human form on Earth who have lived on reptile planets and had that form? Yes.

Do they sometimes have past-life memories from their reptilian lives? Yes.

Has fact and fantasy merged in a lot of people's minds? Yes.

All the energies that contribute to negative feelings within you originate from fear. Left unchecked, negativity will grow, gathering other negative thought and feelings. When people do not understand something, their default is normally to fear it. They then generate negative feelings about the subject and those negative feelings of fear draw in more negative energy. Most negativity thrives in some hypothetical future instead of the present.

What should you do? Live in the moment, being observant of all around you. Choose to allow only positive thoughts to inhabit your world, and all of this will cease to concern you.

Chapter Eight
Psychic contact

The Masters have a lot to say about our psychic experiences. They encourage those with psychic ambitions and counsel those wishing to contact the Spirit World, outlining some of the events in the life of people who are open to spiritual experience, and warning them against possible dangers and difficulties.

Enhancing psychic abilities
Open invitation to spirits
Being aware of spirits
Accuracy in answers
Energy orbs
Negativity shields
Near-death experiences
Holiday visits by spirits
Contacting the departed
Out-of-body experiences
Opening a dialogue
Poisoning thoughts
Unwelcome experiences
Non-physical contacts
Flying solo
A soul's nighttime activities

Enhancing psychic abilities

We get asked this question in many different forms: Which way to train as a psychic is correct? Who is the best person to help me? How do I access my gifts? What do I need to do to increase my abilities? The answer is different for each individual.

Each soul is on a personal path, able to hear, feel, and see things in its own unique way. When you go out to purchase a new vehicle you start by asking yourself a bunch of questions. What do I want to use it for? What do I want it to look like? How much am I able to spend? How large does it need to be to fulfill my needs? What type of engine do I want to have? What mileage is the minimum that I want to receive? How many people does it need to accommodate? Only after deciding the answers do you know where to begin your search.

When it comes to healing and psychic abilities, you need to define for yourself what you feel is the direction you wish to take. In the healing field, do you want to do hands-on healing like massage therapy or acupuncture, or do you want to do energetic work like Reiki or chakra balancing, or do you prefer therapy through hypnosis? Psychically, do you feel called to do work helping physical or non-physical beings? Do you want to locate water, minerals, or missing people? Or is the importance for you being able to communicate with your guides and the ascended ones?

Once you have defined your goal, you read, question, and open yourself to the energy of any person or program that is appealing to you. Some of the teachers who are out there are trying to make a living from their abilities, so they will be like any good salesperson and try to tell you why their product is the best. Just as single people do not need huge SUVs or gas-guzzling trucks for basic transportation, those simply wishing to learn about themselves through communication with their guides do not have to go through multiple stages of a healing-school curriculum to speak to them in meditation.

When you know what you want, open up your energy and feel what each person you talk to, or brochure you read, is saying about your path. Is it resonating with you? Do you get that warm, gushy feeling that you are being loved and hugged by the energy? If so, then jump on board because it will take you for the ride you are seeking.

Open invitation to spirits

When mediums establish contact with non-physicals, most protect themselves and those with them by asking to make contact only with energies that will come for the highest and greatest good. With protection in place, discarnates (*souls who have left their physical bodies but have not transitioned Home*) may not come on their own and may only answer questions directly put to them. They do not have carte blanche to come and stay.

People who have played around with the Ouija board, with no thought of whom they could be asking into their house, may have attracted a group of spirits who had not gone Home. The spirits may have had too much fun staying inebriated while still alive, so they chose not to leave. They identified with fun times in the house and wanted to relive some of their exploits through the group playing with the board. They were sure to remain around until asked, or helped, to leave.

If you find yourself in such a situation, the easiest way to get them to leave is to rescind the invitation unequivocally. Once invited, to un-invite, you must say so three times. Discarnates also do not like the smell of sage [*used frequently by American Indians and others to clear unwanted spirits from locations*]. If none of these things works, try contacting a local channeler or medium to talk to the spirits and find out why they are sticking around.

Being aware of spirits

Souls that are not incarnate are in energetic form and may appear to float as they move around. As they move in the atmosphere that you inhabit, they disrupt the air, and then they become visible to the human eye—if you allow yourself to be aware of them. What is necessary for someone to see free souls is, first, a belief that other non-physical souls exist and, second, an acceptance that you can see them.

We are very pleased that your media has given more people a greater understanding of the basic principles of soul life, through your various television series. Ghosts, reincarnation, animal communication, voices from beyond— all these experiences are becoming commonplace to you, opening your perspective to possibilities.

All souls exist at Home in unconditional love. When you are happy it brings in more love—love of self, love of life, love of others—and that draws more souls to help you share and celebrate love. Practice living in love and we will always be there to rejoice with you.

Accuracy in answers

There are hundreds of different applications of physical tools that can be used to understand and bring through metaphysical information from the non-physical aspects. The use of each comes with the accuracy level of the practitioners. If the users are open and have no pre-conceived notions of what the results should be, they have the option of receiving accurate information.

Those who are using any of the various psychic tools should not be concerned with the answers or material coming through, because it should not be coming from them but from the Other Side. Only if they are influencing the results in some way, as with their own beliefs, should they worry about what they are saying. The reading can only be what the energy is tending toward at that moment, and if people change their direction, either out of choice or after hearing the reading, the results will change. That is not the "fault" of the psychic and does not make the reading incorrect at the time it was given.

Information that comes through should be used for advice only and not as the definitive word on the issue. Freedom of choice should still be used by all. You should always follow what feels right under the circumstances. It is best to stick with one or two methods since ease of getting the messages comes with continued use. As with any activity, whether it be accounting, cooking, or an athletic sport, it is necessary to practice to perfect the art.

Practice at every opportunity, even asking yourself yes and no questions about who is the next to call you, or what the weather will be like. You have to become tuned into the energy in order to read it. You will be ready to move on when you feel comfortable with change and a new endeavor. Don't try to rush things.

Energy orbs

In most cases visitors from the Other Side take the shape of a shimmering sphere of swirling energy. It is very difficult for most people to see these orbs in person, but they are easily captured on a digital camera and sometimes even on film. Souls take many forms, but the most common are spheres that appear to have geometric shapes within them; these shapes are one of our means of communication. Sometimes the soul will take the time to form an appearance similar to a human face. Occasionally several souls will band together and you will be able to detect several different energies within a single orb.

For those of you who have never noticed energy orbs before, it is the Earthly form that we take when we are visiting in your time and dimension without bothering to formulate what approximates to a physical body. If an area contains happy or very spiritual energy such as may be caused by energy healing, meditation, or chakra balancing, we come for enjoyment and to share with the human beings there.

A few souls who have the ability to see auras will be able to see us out of the corner of their eyes. We are most easily seen in digital camera images because our energy vibration registers in the pixels. Regular film is not as sensitive and will rarely detect us. As guides we are around you all the time, and this is one way you may be able to verify our existence if you really need to do so. We feel like saying, "Tag, you're it! Catch us if you can."

Negativity shields

The physical world that you currently inhabit is grounded on the basis of a duality: for all the positive energy there is an equal amount of negative energy. Most people are never aware of the sensation of a positive or negative force around them. As people begin to clear away their life lessons, which are experiences dealing with negativity, they become aware of positive energy, which is the absence of negativity.

Once people have felt positive energy, they want to increase the amount around them. Even if they have never realized the feel of positive energy, they sense the lightness or shimmering of positive energy and want to embrace it. This energy is like a beacon that draws moths to its light— others cannot avoid its appeal.

When souls have newly completed their lessons and positive energy comes in, generally they are not able to sense when others come along and try to steal it; they are just aware that one moment they feel fine and the next they are exhausted. We have a name for people who come along searching for and stealing positive energy: "energy vampires."

It is possible to steal energy from souls only if they allow it to happen. The permission may be an open invitation to share or simply a thought of "I feel so great—can you feel it?" Any little hint that you don't mind your energy being taken away is considered an invitation to come in and snack.

To prevent your providing "tasty morsels" for other souls, you need the intention to keep what is yours to yourself, unless you actually decide to share. All you need to do is to say to the universe [to all energies everywhere] that you do not want to share your energy. You can also envision yourself protected by a barrier of white light, ask your guides to protect you, or simply say, "No sampling without my permission."

Holiday visits by spirits

The energetic excitement on planet Earth can be felt in the ether or on the Other Side, as we refer to it, with an intensity that creates vibrations that can't be ignored. Each soul has its own distinct vibrational pattern, just as each body has its own vocal identity. If you are excited, particularly in the extremes of happiness, anticipation, and love, it's like sending out invitations to those who once had contact with you, to celebrate a special event.

You may enjoy the company of friends and relatives around the holidays for whom you don't have time during the rest of the year. Your deceased friends and relatives relish the opportunity to share being not only with you but with the rest of the group that you have gathered around you.

Even during the times when you are alone, you will have memories of your dear departed. These thoughts send an invitation to them to share the love of your feelings for them. They like nothing better than curling up next to you or across from you as you think about them—while they send you the sense of their love and presence. Enjoy their visit!

Contacting the departed

Some transitional spirits, who have left their physical body but have not let loose completely of the contact with their Earthly life, try to interact with living people.

In most cases the souls do not fully accept that they have left their physical body, and wish to stay on Earth. We call these souls "discarnates." Most died with some very strong emotion firing within them. They may have been outraged at the reason for their death or the person responsible for it. They may feel they have information that will allow those they left behind to deal better with their passing. Revenge, greed, hatred, and control issues are all very powerful emotions that may keep a soul from letting go after its life is terminated.

When souls pass out of their physical body they enter an energetic form. Within this framework it is very difficult for them to interact directly with those in physical form. It may, however, be very easy for them to affect the energy surrounding living people to let them know they are still around and even what they want. If they are working with very strong emotions, their energy may be of sufficient strength to be felt. Those who had contact with the departed before transition also may be more susceptible to feeling the energy because they are familiar with the entities' human energy patterns.

Someone who is very sensitive to energy also may be more affected, which makes it seem as if the deceased is physically reaching out from the grave and grabbing the living. Harm may come only if the receiver is open to accepting all aspects of the energy from the discarnate. Instead, the living person may choose only to hear the thoughts and may block the strong, harmful emotions attached.

Your loved ones do wish to maintain contact and to reassure you that they are happy and content at Home. Frequently they will use their energy to give you clues, such as sounds, smells, or even a disturbance of the air around you that feels just like a caress. You are encouraged to speak to them just as you did when you could physically see them—they will hear you and they still love you.

Out-of-body experiences (OBEs)

Out-of-body experiences happen when people's consciousness is focused on another location or time, and they are able to see everything that is going on in that separate location while their physical bodies remain "at home." They happen in states of deep meditation, and sometimes at night at the beginning or end of the sleep cycle.

OBEs are very real. Individuals who have experienced them can tell you (while physically not leaving their meditation or bedroom) what someone was wearing or what someone said on the other side of a wall, the country, or the world. The reason is simply that these people have grown to know their soul well enough to free the majority of it from the confines of the body. An OBE may also occur when a person is in a coma.

Mystics have meditated for years and not been able to accomplish an OBE, and yet other souls do it almost automatically. The secret is having total faith in yourself as a soul while harboring no fears whatsoever. Doubt, fear, and physical discomfort will drop the soul back into the body immediately. It is impossible to get stuck outside your body.

Near-death experiences (NDEs)

Near-death experiences most often occur when human beings experience a traumatic event that allows their soul (together with its consciousness) to almost completely exit the body—just leaving the tiniest filament connected to their physical body. It is at this time that some souls make the decision to return Home.

The people you have heard speak of their NDEs are those who, at the moment of evaluation—the "go/no-go" point—exercise their freedom of choice to return to their bodies and carry on with their current life. This decision may be made after conferring with relatives and friends who have passed over, and who meet them in the "tunnel" connecting the physical with the spiritual dimensions.

When people start to reach into that space between the dimensions, their perception is determined by the prior experiences and energetic connections that are most important to them at that moment. They may see what their current life is really like, and how closely they are intertwined with other people, and may assess what effect their leaving at this time would have upon those others. They are likely to see just about anything that will help them to choose whether to continue going Home, or to stay on Earth and finish what they have started. Their destination is always wholly a matter for their free choice.

Most people have these NDEs because they are at a crossroads in their life and need new direction. They may even have had an NDE arranged for their present life as a reminder of why they are in that life and what they wanted to do when they came down to Earth. Some people have made arrangements to have an NDE occur if they ever spin out of control. (Their "death" may result from an accidental overdose, a car accident, carbon monoxide inhalation, or the like.)

One thing that occurs almost one hundred percent of the time after an NDE is that the people are changed. They are more connected to their feelings, more introspective, more aware in the spiritual sense. You will always know when you have had one, unless you consciously suppress the memory because you don't want to face what it presented to you.

You do not have to have a NDE in order to know yourself. Simply meditate and connect with the stillness inside of you, and get to the point where you regularly contact your guides to help find the answers to the same questions that present themselves during an NDE.

Opening a dialogue

A lady entered a graveyard to take digital photos. Spirits and cloudlike masses appeared on the photos. Then something destroyed the camera. After this she started seeing colored orbs, faces, people, babies in bonnets, and soldiers in uniform. Then she heard voices: some of them were kind, others said they were demonic. She stopped dialoguing with them and now totally refuses to tune in to them.

It is possible to open a dialogue with souls that are stuck between the physical dimension and the comfort of Home where all souls reside. When the lady entered the graveyard she did so with a curiosity about what she could discover. She asked the universe, "What's here?" and it showed her. She extended an invitation to the souls to make themselves visible to her. This is a doorway between the dimensions.

These souls were trying to get answers for their current state of affairs. Some were unaware that they had passed away and needed to be helped to understand that they could go home. Those that followed the lady are the ones that were bored hanging around the graves and used her to see something new. Some of these souls were just confused and meant no harm, and some were negative forces that wished to control and create fear.

The energy orbs are something different. They are the form that souls who are already at Home use to be seen on Earth. They have a very positive and loving energy. Some of them try to help lost souls go Home. Observers have no obligation to have anything to do with these souls. If you have an unwelcome experience with them, you may start by telling them that they are uninvited from interacting with you. If you wish to help any of the souls, you may direct them to find the light and follow it back Home. The negative souls want energy from you and it would take some work to get them to move on.

White-gold light is the light of Home. You may envision it as surrounding yourself and those around you. Negativity cannot pass through a strong shell of this light. You may also ask your personal guides to assist these lost souls on their voyage Home.

Poisoning thoughts

How much of your time do you spend wishing something would happen or become true? You send thoughts out to those around you, trying to influence the flow of the energy coming to you. Some souls have a very strong, forceful flow of intention moving out from them. This is like a person with a powerful voice that may be heard over a great distance.

It is always possible for people to attempt to influence you. Every day, friends tell you what they think about the way you are doing something. Some try intimidation to get you to accept their ideas. The media constantly implants thoughts in your head about products to purchase which they say you cannot live without.

Regardless of where the thoughts come from—a well-meaning friend, a marketing company, or someone who seeks to destroy your energy—what happens is up to you. In each of these cases the effort to shape you must stand up to your freedom of choice to make it a part of your consciousness.

All these influences become part of your belief system. If you accept blindly what is inside your head, implanted from the outside, you are saying that those ideals should control your actions. If, instead, you unconsciously question everything that you do to see if it is really what you want to do, then you are controlling yourself. No one can control you without your permission. That does not stop someone from trying. Just deflect their shouting and make your own decisions.

Unwelcome experiences

There are two causes for the feeling that people can experience of having an attachment. The first is the presence of a discarnate soul who has left its human body but has not moved back Home to unconditional love. These souls generally stick around because of their desire for revenge, their hatred of a particular person, a love they do not want to leave, their fear of the afterlife, or love of the power of the negative. They do not care how much they affect a person, and they even become empowered by the fear of their victim.

They are attracted to a particular person to get even or cause havoc or, more simply, because they are confused. They perceive that an invitation of some sort was given to them by the victim. This may have been a direct statement made in ignorance: "I wish I knew what it was like to be a ghost." "I wish Bert were still here." The invitation also could have been issued in a semi-waking state at the end of a dream cycle. To revoke the visitor's permit, one must tell the discarnate in no uncertain terms to depart.

The second circumstance in which these sensations may occur is an out-of-body experience. At night you do not remain in your body; you leave a tiny connection to keep your body alive and then you go traveling. While the majority of your soul is out of your body it is communicating with other souls, friends, and advisors.

It is a frequent occurrence, especially when the body is awakened abruptly by a sound, that the conscious mind returns to the site of the body but does not enter it before there is awareness. The conscious mind is trying to get the physical body to move but the energy pack, the soul, has not been replaced and so the body cannot move. You are still more in a non-physical state than a physical one, so you are still able to apprehend communication from the Other Side. The words are not in language your human body can understand because spirits do not have vocal cords.

Experiencing this can be very frightening. You are unable to control your body, feeling that it is held down. You are in between two dimensions and your conscious mind is expecting just the usual physical surroundings. If this ever happens to you, relax—do not fight the sensations; observe what is occurring and you will become aware of your reentry into your body. When you are comfortable with this procedure you may even use it to travel out of body while you are awake. Many people have spent decades trying to do this!

Non-physical contacts

Souls currently in human form may be affected by discarnates—those who leave their body but don't return Home. Everything is composed of energy, and souls wandering between the physical and their true essence need to find ways to replenish the energy they are using to stay between energetic layers. The only way they can get energy is by sucking it from those in full physical form. Many refer to these lost souls as energy vampires or spiritual leeches.

Souls who are working on finding their true essence, called "lightworkers," emanate a high level of energy that is preferred by vampires. If you are a lightworker, consider yourself a beacon that may be seen from a great distance. Like moths drawn to a flame they cannot resist, vampires are drawn to your energy. Your awareness of self allows you to keep them from attaching permanently, but they come and feed at times. Start the practice of surrounding your body in white-gold light at least once a day. The vampires will not be able to see you in this glare and will get discouraged from not being able to get a free meal.

Flying solo

When you were young you didn't have a belief system that told you traveling outside of your body was impossible. You still had some of the memories from when you were at Home. You knew, at your soul level, how to transport yourself wherever you wished to be. You also yearned for the sensation of total freedom and being able to fly.

As you got older (in Earth terms), you forgot the marvelous sensations and possibilities. Society's belief, which says that human bodies are solid masses that cannot divide and separate, took control. You no longer believed that you could fly, so you didn't.

Now you may be opening yourself up to all eventualities, putting aside what was programmed into you, and attempting to rewrite what feels right to you, but you still haven't returned to that childlike stage. That state of unlimited possibilities exists in faith—the faith that children have that what they feel is what they can do. Return to that unconditional faith in your inner feelings, your soul, and you will be able to fly.

Your entire soul does not remain in your body at all times. Always a portion of it is at Home in the energy of unconditional love, but during your wakefulness, the majority is within your conscious body. In order for bodies to be viable, each must have an attachment to a soul, but the majority of the soul can be elsewhere.

At night, your soul goes on various expeditions, visiting your guides and teachers and other souls who are part of your soul group. You also go to consult your akashic [celestial] records (where you have recorded all the lessons that you learned in other lifetimes), so that you can determine if you will need some of that past wisdom during your present life. Occasionally you may be aware of some of these happenings as you recall them in dreams.

You may have gone off with a large chunk of your soul because you have multiple or complicated tasks to perform. Then, should you begin to wake up before your body has acclimated to the return of your essence, and not enough of your nerves have become active again, you will be fully conscious but physically unable to move your body until the "juice" has permeated throughout your cells. It is nothing to be concerned about. Try to recall what was happening just before you awakened. You may find it interesting.

A soul's nighttime activities

While the physical body needs time to rest and rejuvenate, the soul does not. To sit all night inside a body that is unconscious is wasted time, so your soul goes visiting. Sometimes you will visit friends, other times relive a section of a prior life or try out an experience that you have observed others having.

Your higher self is the unconscious aspect of the human body that contains your memories and history of experiences. These experiences include things that your body has done or observed. These observations may be of actual occurrences or ones recorded by others, including movies, novels, and the imaginings told you by these people. The physical experiences are also contained within the brain.

The body may be involved in one activity while your higher self is involved in another. Your mind may be replaying a sporting event you participated in, while your higher self is learning about expressing unconditional love in various ways. Since the mind is in control of the physical body, its activities may be reflected in motion within the body while mostly asleep. This may be movement such as walking, or it may involve a talking out of the situation the mind is working through.

Spirit World Wisdom

Chapter Nine
Interesting Information

In the course of the three years writing their blog, the Spirit Masters have dealt with a number of interesting subjects from Twin Flames (generally misunderstood) to the relations that human beings have with their pets, and issues relating to crime.

Twin flames
Astrology and soul mates
Human templates
Amnesia is a tool
Wanting to be alone
Halloween
Pets reflecting ourselves
Dreaming pets
Do dolphins have souls?
Sexual abuse and clergy
Is the death penalty murder?
Serial killers
Crime and the energy shift
Judgment

Twin flames

We need to make clear the difference between twin flames and soul mates. Many of you ask about twin flames or twin souls. Others use this term to refer to a physically romantic relationship that is particularly intense. We only use this term to refer to the last energetic fragment of Source that broke off at the same time as your soul.

Twin flames are like Siamese twins. Let us explain that statement. The last division that occurred, when Source created you as an individual soul, took place between you and the energy known as your "twin flame." It is the only soul who can make you feel complete, because it was once an intimate part of you.

If both you and your twin flame are in body form at the same time and meet each other, you will immediately seek to spend all your time together because you feel whole for the first time. Most of the time twin souls do not make arrangements to meet on Earth because all they would be concerned with is each other and they would not get to the learning of their lessons.

Now that you have decided to incarnate and spend time on planet Earth, meeting that spark ignites all the old memories within you of Home and of the magnificent unconditional love. Coming into contact with a twin soul is shocking to the physical being because it stimulates spontaneously all the non-physical abilities you two have previously shared. You want to spend time with each other and do nothing but exist in each other's presence. For this reason, twin souls rarely plan to spend time together while experiencing Earth.

Soul mates are all the souls who were created as individuals about the same moment as you. Think of an extended family tree: These souls would be your parents, grandparents, siblings, and cousins if you all were to incarnate at the same time. These are the souls with whom

144

you make your most important contracts before you incarnate.

You do, however, choose to spend a good amount of time with members of what we call your soul group. This group numbers up to 144, but you have intimate relations with only about 12 to 24 of them. This is roughly the equivalent of an extended human family. They all came into being at about the same time that you did, and you spend the majority of your lifetimes fulfilling contracts with them to help you learn your desired lessons. These are the souls with whom you make all your major contracts before coming to Earth. You have been with them many times and they know you the best.

You trust your soul mates with ensuring that you will experience exactly what you chose. These are not just immediate human family members and spouses, but also that teacher who influenced your career path, or the drunk driver who handicapped you so that you might experience helplessness. Because you frequently spend time on Earth with these same souls during different incarnations, whenever you meet one of them, immediately he or she will seem familiar to you. Be aware of this contact. See where it can lead you and what adventures together it brings you. Enjoy!

Astrology and soul mates

Astrology, generally recognized as the influence of the planets upon the human body, has been documented throughout human history. The moment of birth gives you an indication of the potential that the incarnated soul has within that particular body. It does not determine what is going to happen to that person, just what the energy background will help to facilitate.

Souls may take their initial potential, determined by the planets at the time of their birth, and ride along with it without making any changes, or use it as a springboard to propel themselves beyond their natural inclinations in a direction of their choosing. They would appear then to differ greatly from others of their astrological sign.

Throughout your planet, with its population of billions, there are many people who are born on each of your Earth days. Take for instance your large women's hospitals that specialize in maternity care; every day perhaps a dozen babies are born in each.

When you consider that we generally make contracts, and come to planet Earth, with no more than a dozen or so of our soul mates, it is easy to see why a shared birth date does not indicate the co-existence of a soul mate. It is not impossible but very improbable—unless the other person is an identical twin with whom you sought to spend an entire lifetime. But that does not mean twins are always soul mates, either.

Human templates

The human fetus has a DNA template provided by the biological parents whom it has chosen. This DNA supplies physical, ethnic, medical, and physical sensitivities and propensities to the developing body shell. The soul has its own history, carried in its DNA, which is created by the previous life experiences recorded in the akashic records.

The physical DNA characteristics are imprinted within the physical body, while the historic DNA is in the etheric body and may be called into play, or not, as the soul sees fit during its lifetime. These both may act as blueprints for the development of the person, depending upon the soul's freedom of choice for the experiences being sought.

There is a third thing that can come into play in determining characteristics and afflictions, based upon the soul's freedom to call things to itself through its intention. When something is desired that is not already part of its blueprint from parents or from past history, the soul rewrites its blueprint, with its intention to change the direction in which it is heading.

For instance, a soul may have a propensity to be addicted because its biological blueprint is for an addictive personality, and it has had past lives as a drunk and an obsessive compulsive. But as this person grows up, that addictive personality realizes that he (or she) is destructively addictive because he never wanted to take responsibility for his actions and was running away. He then develops a strong sense of self-worth and responsibility for every aspect of his life and, through intention, rewrites the blueprint: he is now a well-balanced, non-addicted, responsible individual.

Amnesia is a tool

Souls don't always come down to a new incarnation with total amnesia of their past exploits. The only thing they absolutely don't remember is anything that might prevent them from learning all the different aspects of the lessons planned for this particular life.

A teacher will not give a student the answers to the exam before she has taught the class, because the students would not pay any attention to the lessons and therefore would not learn anything new. So it is with life lessons. If you know what you are going to learn through an experience, and it has anything you might consider unpleasant, you are not going to go ahead and subject yourself to the situation.

Frequently it takes more than one lifetime to complete a particular task. When you must start at the beginning each time, you find different and, potentially, better ways to complete the necessary activities with each retake of the lesson. Knowing beforehand what will come might speed things up, but you are more likely to merely repeat the beginning of the failed lesson rather than trying a new approach, because you have done it before.

Amnesia presents an opportunity to go into your feelings and sense the most beneficial way to do something instead of going into your head and seeing what previous experiences you have stored there.

Wanting to be alone

Every soul is on its own journey. You come to Earth to be able to experience the duality or negativity available nowhere else. For most souls those lessons will include contracts made with other people, and therefore it is necessary for you to interact with others in order to complete your tasks.

However, each soul is on Earth for itself, not for the benefit of someone else. There are individual lessons that you are here to understand. So if you are working on an issue of self-worth, self-love, or any of the human emotions that you have carried over from a past incomplete lifetime, solitude is the best way to work on your journey without interference from other people.

Tom Hanks's character in the movie *Castaway* was thrown into a situation where he had to face himself. Did he value his life enough to keep fighting with his inner demons and with his physical environment? When the thought of ending it all took over for a while, his subconscious kept putting up obstacles and giving him reasons to live. He would not have grown in the self-acceptance and inner peace that he took away from the island if other people had been around.

Some of you have chosen to have lifetimes in which you can advance your wisdom only when you are alone to work on your fears and doubts, which are the outward personification of your chosen life lessons. Society around you is begging you to return and interact so it can have the benefit of your hard work. Believe in what your intuition is telling you to do. Mystics of your past history followed their inner feelings and knew that, for them, the way to enlightenment was a solitary journey.

Halloween

You have a festival on Earth called All Hallows Eve or Halloween. To many it merely signals the change from summer into winter, a last chance before cold sets in for the children to have a romp outside. It is an opportunity to gather a horde of goodies for the winter just as the squirrels are preparing their winter stashes. Mirth and trick-or-treating is the assignment of the day. It is acceptable to dress up or disguise yourself so that you may play pranks on people without their knowing your true identity. You may be queen for a day, a pirate, or an alien— anything but what you are in real life. It is a chance to step out of yourself and seemingly not be responsible for your actions. For adults, it is a reverting back to their carefree childhoods where they can still dream of being a fireman or a ballet dancer.

But there is another reason to celebrate this day. The true origin of Halloween was to acknowledge and honor the spirit, a remembrance of all the physical lives and experiences your souls have led on Earth. It was also a time to aid any soul that might be stuck on the physical plane to go into the Light (return Home). People went in search of wayward souls and with compassion helped them understand they were no longer physical and were free to move on with no further Earth obligations.

Your media, which likes to sensationalize everything to sell itself, has taken this honorable task, switched the roles, and "villainized" the action. The poor, stuck souls have turned into horrible, mindless, stalking images that roam the surface looking for unsuspecting humans to prey upon—to turn them into ghouls after sucking out their blood for nourishment! Halloween has become a time for frightening little children and for teens to see how brave they are.

Reflect on these thoughts. Let this be a day to renew your life's mission of learning lessons. Remember that all those who have gone before you were trail-blazing the pathways back home. The day following All Hallows Eve is called All Saints Day in many Christian denominations. Take a moment to reflect particularly upon those who have returned Home, both relatives and friends, who played a part in your own experience. Thank the teachers who had agreed to be here with you to keep you on your pre-determined track, but have now moved on. Celebrate the whole cycle of the soul, from Home to Earth to Home again, with a sense of gratitude.

Pets reflecting ourselves

The animals that you choose to raise as pets serve you in many ways. In the case of a lonely person, pets substitute for human companionship. If you have very little self-confidence, you find pets non-threatening, contrary to people. When you lose one of them, that portion of love in your life is removed, and as much as it hurts to lose a pet, you need to have that love replaced, so you get another pet.

Interaction with pets also reflects the personality of the owner. It represents one's innermost thoughts, feelings, and needs. Most people have pets to provide the love that they cannot get in any other way. Pets, particularly dogs, love their owners unconditionally, regardless of how they are treated. Who doesn't want to be adored by someone or something? Other people need to have control, to be able to strike out at something, to get revenge for hurt suffered without having to deal with the cause of the hurt.

Dysfunctional people (in human terms) who cannot deal with others can still satisfy their need to control by training their animals to do what they desire. Seeing that something obeys every command gives a sense of worth to the individual who has a feeling of being worthless. Even having a fish, which eagerly comes to the top of the bowl to get fed, feels good to the lonely and provides the idea of being in control of at least a part of his or her world.

Animals can also keep an elderly person young. They provide a reason to get up and move, to feed, exercise, and take care of the pet friend. They keep loneliness at bay, and are a great way to meet others who share an interest in a similar type of pet.

Because pets do not have the longevity of humans, you are forced to see them come and go while you stay around. This allows you to take stock of how your former pet assisted you with your life's lessons, and gives you the opportunity to try a new approach to further your growth within a new relationship.

Dreaming pets

Some animals travel out of their body at night. The soul inhabiting your pet retains memories of other experiences just like a human soul. They like to go and visit other places and other times.

Not all of the activity that you may notice has to do with outside movement. Animals also dream just as you do. When they are dreaming they cannot tell that they are not awake, so they react to the activity. It is very similar to humans' walking, talking, or crying out during sleep.

The more active animals are during their awake time, the more active they are during their sleep time. As pets get older, and have difficulty moving, their sleep activity sometimes means that they are reliving the glories and triumphs from their prime, and their degenerating bodies don't exist in those memories.

Do dolphins have souls?

Dolphins, as you know, are mammals. They were once walking on the surface of the planet before they chose to go into the sea. They have brains that are comparable to humans' in size, and they use a larger portion of their brain than humans do. A large number of souls who choose to have inter-species experiences have chosen to experience them in the body of a dolphin.

The majority of dolphins on the planet today have only a spark of life, the same as other mammals like lions, dogs, and apes. There are inbred in a number of species the need to protect humans from themselves and dangerous situations. It has become instinctual in their nature.

Dolphins are extremely gregarious animals, fun loving and protective of their pod. A person in the water can easily become a thing of interest or a playmate. There are a lot of recorded instances of dolphins supporting injured humans or other mammals such as small whales or even seals until they can reach a place of safety. There are also reports from those who spend a lot of time in the water with wild dolphins that, on occasion, they have been attacked by dolphins when their activity has been perceived as threatening, such as getting too close to a mother birthing or a tiny newborn.

Family pets, whether dog, cat, or even birds, will come to the aid of their owners in a time of crisis such as medical emergency or during an accident such as a fire. These occurrences are not the result of training or instinct but arise from a sense of love or companionship. Dogs will frequently help injured or lost children and sometimes other animals. Apes have adopted and raised similar species and even humans who have become lost or stranded in the wild. The mothering instinct of mammals is species blind.

Sexual abuse and clergy

Each soul chooses in advance the lessons that it wishes to experience during a particular lifetime. It may well be as the abused or as the abuser. You selected the situation and made the contracts to enable your teaching to take place. Most cases of abuse are about learning the limits of your own power, self-worth, strength, and choices.

The lesson is much more powerful in the climate of a religion because it also has overtones of faith, trust, and the sense of betrayal. One of the first elements of society that contributes to the belief system by which you live your life is the faith within which you are raised. Your parents presented their religion to you as a place as safe for you as they themselves—presided over by an ever-loving God who protects you.

Under this seemingly protective bubble, children do what they are told without ever questioning. It is not until later, when outside influences let them know that inappropriate behavior has occurred, that doubts, fears, and anxieties begin.

Children first blame themselves for questioning the behavior of the trusted clergy, frequently having their parents call them liars for accusing such a pious person. When the accusations surface, there may be condemnation of the children by the rest of the members of the church, who believe them to be incorrect. Unless the children can connect with their inner strength, power, self-worth, and purpose, they are crippled for life.

You must realize that "God" has nothing to do with these lessons. Each soul has total freedom of choice. Pedophiles are living their own hell on Earth, as are the victims, until each awakens to the lesson within. On the soul level, they are assisting each other in their progress. At Home there will be thanks all around for the assistance given. If you hold on to the negativities—anger, guilt, hatred, loathing, inability to forgive—you will remain stuck and will be unable to move away from that lesson and on to your next.

Is the death penalty murder?

We do not judge the things that you souls decide to experience and experiment with while you are in body form. All souls, whether you perceive them as "good guys" or "bad guys", are the same on the soul level. You all were broken off from Source and contain the same unconditionally loving energy. Only on Earth is there negativity. Only there do you react in an emotional way to "justice" – because it only exists on Earth.

Regardless of how the incarnate soul is attired, as saint or sinner per Earth standards, he is obliged to follow the rules and regulations where he chose to live. If he is trying out the energy of a murderer, and he did so in an area that upholds the death penalty, he was aware of that on a soul level when he planned the life. The experience of the execution may have been the reason he chose the drama involved.

Many nations and areas on the planet do not allow executions within their judicial systems, the vast majority because they feel carrying out the sentence would make them murderers. They feel that the prisoner should spend time repenting. But it is impossible to force another to do anything they do not seek to do. The inmate may spend the rest of his time on Earth cursing the system and the world, and spewing gross negativity into the area.

Forced time alone, possibly resulting in the discovery of meditation, may aid a soul in working through the life lessons for which it came to Earth. That also would have been part of the plan. Working through life lessons might also happen to the soul when it is faced with imminent death. But we inquire: How do you save a person who has established another direction for life and is not prepared to be saved?

Serial killers

When a massive number of people are involved in a transition back Home, it has an effect upon the whole planet. Hitler, certainly, was part of a very notorious movement during your recent history. Other notable mass events include Rwanda, Chechnya, the 2004 tsunami, the twin towers, and many earthquakes, landslides, fires, and floods. All of these events were for the entire planet to take note and be affected accordingly.

There have been a number of souls who contracted to be the source of transition for multiple souls, but not to be an impact on a global level. These serial killers have a life lesson of being without feelings or conscience, and either are unable to control their urges or are truly "evil" as modern society judges its people. These souls are not intended to have any particular effect upon all souls currently sharing life, but only upon the victims, families, and pursuers. These are individual lessons for each one of them.

These killers would have gone unnoticed to the majority of mankind but for the fact that murder sells and makes the media salivate. More than one violent crime committed by a single soul becomes a series, and reporters all try to out-shock each other and the public.

For those not directly involved there is no lesson except that you should not judge. Merely evaluate this behavior as you do any other acts that represent a soul's life lessons. [*The Masters are not saying that incarcerating serial killers is not socially necessary.*]

Crime and the energy shift

The current energy of the planet is interesting to observe. People had lost connection with their neighbors and lived their own lives away from their neighborhood and city. As financial fears have set in, they are staying closer to home and are getting acquainted or reacquainted with their neighbors. They are attending functions close to home, and establishing a feeling of belonging and responsibility.

When you feel isolated from others you don't care what is happening to them or to their property. The only important thing is that which affects you directly. With the closeness caused by the fear to venture forth, the range of sight has been restricted. Your neighborhood is now the same as your own house; your city has become your neighborhood. People are stepping up and watching and caring for others, and this is creating a "crime watch," which results in a crime-free zone because the criminals sense the vigilance. Neighbor is helping neighbor, so that sense of desperation is alleviated. Would-be thieves are being helped by new friends. Potential drug addicts are getting help from family and friends. Communities are beginning to raise the children again. And the largest change is the energy that prevails.

As the planets shift in the cosmos, the energy is shifting to a lightness and clearness enabling souls to tap into the higher non-physical dimensions, if they so choose. Even those people who are not working on their spiritual paths feel the lessening of tension. As the number of lightworkers who are approaching awareness of self increases, the force of positive thought will predominate over negative thought. All can help in this shift by holding positive intentions for themselves and for the planet.

Judgment

Judgment occurs when the human ego feels compelled to assess everything as right or wrong, or to grade people or actions as better or worse than other people or their actions. Someone who evaluates himself according to a standard of society—or, as a matter of pride, decides he is better than another human—is exhibiting judgment. If, on the other hand, he makes an observation about a person's trait but makes no determination of the trait's rightness or wrongness, he is noting what he sees without going into judgment.

Our answers are simply descriptions of people about whom we are asked—a matter of identification. We do not judge the merit of their traits but merely, by identifying them, enable the [people asking us questions] to decide [what to do]. Frequently, people on the spot cannot see what is happening around them and need an outside perspective for clarification.

When you make decisions for yourself, you are using your freedom of choice about what direction to try at that time. You are not judging something as wrong based on society's opinions, but just going with your gut feeling that it is not the best thing for you. If, however, you act based on what you think others would want or expect you to do, you are relying on your ego and judgment to make decisions.

You can tell the difference by examining whether you are making the decisions based upon: (a) your thinking—your hard-drive mind supplied with information solely by those outside of you, or (b) your feelings, which rely on your own internal information.

Chapter Ten
Affirmations

The Masters have given us this set of affirmations

I affirm that I will:

Become aware of my true nature.

Love all souls, even those whose choice of lessons does not appeal to me.

Fully accept myself as I am, which is necessary for my chosen path.

Learn to banish fear so I can see the lesson within.

Understand my chosen lessons.

Trust the universe, knowing it will not send me more than I can endure.

Know I create my own reality and have the power to meet all my needs.

Release my ego to fully enjoy my soul's unconditional love.

Commune daily in love with my soul's companions.

Have faith in myself because I am divine.

The Masters' Commentary

We were chuckling to ourselves when we dictated the list of affirmations to our channel Toni. This short selection, with a few minor additions, encompasses the entirety of the Earth experience for the soul. We are happy to make brief comments to assist you.

"To become aware of your true nature" is to connect with the unconditional love that resides within you. It is to be able to feel your soul, your connection to Source and to the universe. With this knowledge also comes the ability to access what has come before in other incarnations, realized by knowledge from your akashic record. Many refer to this as the awakening of the soul within the human body.

"To love all souls sharing this journey with you even when you do not like the nature of their chosen path" is a realization that each soul has freedom of choice and chooses what to experience. Within these choices are a lot of things considered negative within the realm of Earth. No one likes the dictator, the egotist, or the controller if they impact one's life. You must get to the point of seeing that their part is simply the choice they made for this lifetime and is not something that is done to give you a bad time. It is one of your contracts to be within their sphere of operation. Remember you are all the same and all from the same Source.

"To accept yourself fully as you are because it is necessary for the path you walk" means that the reality you adopt concerning your physical attributes, and your mental and emotional stabilities, needs to be a reflection of how you appear as judged by your society. Many people who have body weight issues or personality disorders refuse to accept that they have chosen these issues to learn from them.

In order to use obesity or antisocial behavior as a lesson, you must first accept that it is present and, at the moment, who you are. Then you may discover why you wished to learn from this condition, for that is the path you wrote for yourself.

"To learn to banish all fear so you might see the lesson within." The only emotions that exist on Earth are various forms of fear and love. The soul exists in unconditional love. If you give up your power on Earth by embracing fear, you become unable to see anything else. Therefore, you must put aside the fear to see the soul's desired lesson within any situation. Accept that as a soul you are unconditional love.

"To understand the lessons you came to Earth to learn" means first to go through the lesson chosen, and second to take the knowledge of the energies, both positive and negative, that were generated during the lesson. This means to see what effect your actions during the lesson had upon yourself and those who were also a part of the lesson. This finally results in an understanding of the reasons you chose that lesson, which gives you the wisdom of that particular lesson.

"To trust in the universe knowing it will not give you more than you can endure" is an affirmation of the universal law that in order to learn from the Earth experience, you must not be overwhelmed in the process. The universe does not want you spending all your time treading water and not getting anywhere. To obtain the wisdom from a lesson, you must be able to complete it if you give yourself to the experience, accepting responsibility for what you are doing. You are, after all, a part of the universe.

161

"To know you create your own reality, so you have the power to create what you need to complete your journey." Your soul has freedom of choice, which allows you to create any reality you feel is necessary to finish each task you have chosen. With this comes the understanding that it is incumbent upon you to make the required choices and to begin the requisite actions necessary to take you in your desired direction.

"To be able to release the human ego to enjoy fully the unconditional love of soul" acknowledges that the human ego is based in judgment and the soul exists without judgment. Unconditional love is incompatible with judgment situations. Consider love in normal human society ruled by the ego: can it ever be unconditional? Can you unconditionally love a spouse who loves another as much as or more than you? Can you love your abuser, your master, your betrayer unconditionally? Within the ego, because it judges right and wrong, good and bad, poor and better, you will never reach unconditional love.

"To live each day in communion with your fellow souls in unconditional love" shows the ultimate goal for your current lifetime. This destination is to fully recognize not only your soul self in its human body, but all the other souls sharing this Earth trip. When you reach this point in your incarnation, you are able to communicate not only with the physical beings around you but also the non-physical souls in the universe. You have remembered yourself and taken your place within the entirety of existence.

"To have faith in yourself because you are divine" is a statement of fact concerning your essence. To walk easily through your Earth lessons you need to obtain a sense of your soul. Your soul was broken off from Source, and therefore you are also Source. Being Source, who would not have faith in their decisions and conclusions about their experienced lessons? But even if you cannot fully appreciate your divinity, have faith in those feelings that come from within. For inside all dwells the soul, which is who you truly are.

Glossary of terms

(Cross-references are marked *)

Advisor: See, Guide.

Akashic Records: An energetic* library containing a record of all the knowledge* and wisdom* that has been gained through the experiences that souls* have had upon planet Earth. Each soul has its own record of what has transpired throughout each of its incarnations*. The library contains records of everything undertaken by all the souls who have spent time on Earth.

Angel: A human term for a celestial being who, after being separated from Source*, acts as a guide* to those upon Earth, but may or may not at some later time choose to experience a physical shell*.

Archangel: A human term for a celestial being who is very advanced and experienced as a guide*, whose soul* has never incarnated*.

Ascended (Spirit) Masters: Souls* who have incarnated* and have completed all their lessons, allowing them to come into full enlightenment* of their true nature. These souls no longer need to return to Earth for additional learning. They may choose to return if they wish to teach and mentor other souls in human form.

Ascension: The process by which the soul* becomes totally aware of its essence* and can access all the wisdom* that exists everywhere. (This is not a movement of a physical body into a higher dimension*, which never takes place.)

Belief Systems: Thoughts and actions, initially received and copied from parents, religion, and society, that structure a person's behavior. After gaining awareness of itself, a soul* may rewrite or adapt these received beliefs to comply with its own understanding of reality*.

Contracts: Voluntary agreements that souls* make with other souls while at Home* to ensure that they will have the right Earth situation to help them experience the physical lessons they desire.

Council: A group of guides* who help souls* decide what lessons they wish to experience, and who help them make the best use of the lessons they have learned.

Creator: See, Source.

Dimension: A waveband or stratum of vibrational energy. Planet Earth is at the third dimension. Home* is at the fifth and higher dimensions.

Discarnate: A soul* who clings to the physical because it wants to continue with its past life. This soul/body image remains connected to Earth and contacts or haunts those who remain, until it chooses to return Home*.

Ego: A function of the physical conscious mind that employs judgment* and measures how people perceive themselves. It is a template for the soul* to operate in society so that it may learn lessons and gain wisdom. It is a compilation of human belief systems* deemed necessary for a person to exist in a physical body.

Energy, Energetic: (1) The basic component of all that exists. (2) Non-physical vibration of a dimension* higher than the Earth's, used by the spirit world to communicate.

Enlightenment, Enlightened: The state existing when an incarnate soul* comes to full awareness of the fact that it is an immortal soul and recalls all the implications of its essence*, who it is and what it can do.

Essence: The reality of who you are: an eternal part of the God-Force*.

Freedom of Choice: A universal law that says all souls* have the ultimate right to decide exactly what they are going to do while incarnate*. It extends to all aspects of living, from the choice of biological parents, to the lessons they will learn, and the manner and time of their physical death.

God: See, Source.

God-Force: See, Source. Sometimes used as meaning "all souls*."

Guide: A non-physical soul* who makes itself available to help incarnate* souls use their freedom of choice*.

Heaven: See, Home. Also, a state of mind on Earth.

Hell: A state of mind on Earth.

Higher Self: That portion of the incarnate* soul* that may be accessed to gain information.

Home: Not a physical place but an energetic* dimension* of unconditional love and of conscious connection with Source*. It is where each soul* works with its guides* and council*. Every soul who is not incarnated* is consciously within the dimension of Home.

Incarnate: A soul* who has gone down to planet Earth and is now in a physical body.

Judgment: A state of mind existing only in Earth's physical third dimension*. Because of the duality and polarity of the planet, everything has an opposite. Human beings grade all other people by an impression of where they feel the others exist on a personal, ethical, or religious scale of "good" and "bad."

Karma: A term that relates to the effects of an action taken by human beings. Many people use it to explain away what they consider bad experiences that happen to them. This is inaccurate in its application to human experience. The accurate view is solely the energetic* effect of the action taken.

Knowledge: Awareness of facts and principles but not necessarily how to use or apply them in living.

Lessons: The various pre-planned experiences that a soul* has while incarnate* that allow it to gain wisdom*.

Life review: The experience undertaken by a soul* when it returns Home* after an incarnation*, where its council* and guides* help it to discover the wisdom* within the knowledge* it gained during that particular incarnation.

Masters: See, Ascended Masters.

Matrix: An energetic* network of circuits entwining the whole of existence and allowing for an interchange of wisdom* without the need for verbal communication.

Reality: The perception people have of the world around them. It is influenced by their belief systems*, ego*, and the lessons they are learning. It changes from time to time as they change their beliefs.

Reincarnation: The process the soul* uses to experience more lessons to obtain wisdom*. After completing one incarnation*, the soul returns Home* to assess its experiences and to determine what else it wishes to learn. It then reincarnates by entering into a new physical body in order to have further experiences.

Resonance, resonate: Being in a state where what is happening to you is in synchronization with your essence.* In this state the physical, mental, emotional, and spiritual bodies feel at peace and comfortable with their surroundings.

Shell: The living physical structure inhabited by a soul*. No human or animal body can live without some connection to Source*.

Soul Mate: Another soul* who came into being at the same time. There are groups of individual souls, usually numbering 144 in each group. Generally these are the souls with whom you choose to make your most important contracts* prior to incarnation*.

Souls: Individualized pieces of energy* split off by and from Source*, in order to have unique experiences outside

168

the perfect. They are all particles of Source, so each and every soul is also Source. All souls are equal regardless of the human shell* they have chosen to inhabit.

Source: The point of origin of all that is known by human beings, and of all that exists. It is the energy* of unconditional love, the highest vibrational energy anywhere, and is found in everything. The Source makes no judgments* and does not reward or punish souls*.

Transition: The soul's* move from life in the body to life at Home*. Physical death.

Twin Flame: The very last soul* from whom you are separated when your individualization from Source* occurs.

Wisdom: Awareness of the facts and principles of spiritual life with understanding of how to apply them in living.

The Authors

Peter Watson Jenkins, MA (Cantab.), LLB, MH, is an experienced clinical and metaphysical master hypnotist working in past-life regression and spirit release. In the 1960s he studied theology at Cambridge University, England, and served for 21 years in parish ministry. He is the C.E.O. of Celestial Voices, Inc., the publisher of this book and he wrote or edited the books listed below.

Toni Ann Winninger, JD, CH, is well established as a psychic channeler in practice with individuals, and groups large and small. She works in metaphysical hypnotherapy and specializes in spirit release. A Reiki master, she teaches metaphysical subjects and Light Language. Previously she worked for 27 years as a prosecutor in the Chicago area. Toni is President of Celestial Voices, Inc., which promotes the Masters' messages.

Celestial Voices, Inc.

We hope that you found this book a challenge and an inspiration. We are the human "voice" of the Masters of the Spirit World, and promote their messages. Current books are:

How I Died (and what I did next)
The Masters' Reincarnation Handbook: Journey of the Soul
Talking with Leaders of the Past
Talking with Twentieth-Century Women
Talking with Twentieth-Century Men
Healing with the Universe, Meditation, and Prayer
A Conversation about Birth
A Conversation about Death

CelestialVoicesInc.com
ReimcarnationGuide.com
Facebook / Reincarnation Guide

Glossary

Lightning Source UK Ltd.
Milton Keynes UK
UKOW05f0130050414

229449UK00001B/8/P